IS LOVE LOST?

Mosaics in the life of
Jane Doolittle

IS LOVE LOST?

Mosaics in the life of
Jane Doolittle
"Angel Mother"
in a Muslim Land

Elizabeth C. Kay Voorhees

William Carey Library

PASADENA, CALIFORNIA

Published by
William Carey Library
P.O. Box 40129
1705 N. Sierra Bonita Ave.
Pasadena, California 91104

ISBN 0-87808-218-2
LC CIP# 88-051181

Cover art by Sherri Maroofian
Photo of author on back cover by Sharon Villarreal

Printed in the United States of America

JANE DOOLITTLE offers her story
in memoriam
and tribute to her beloved parents,
Mr. and Mrs. Orrin S. Doolittle
who from the very first accepted
her decision to become a missionary and
then to go to the little known land
of Persia, and who through the years
cooperated in every way to encourage
her in her work in Iran.

Elizabeth K. Voorhees thinks of
the young who follow in her immediate
family: Debriana and her Juli;
Sharon and her Joe Jr.; Sharon Marie
and her Elizabeth; Richard, Helen and
Alice; trusting that "... in all things
He may have the preeminence ..." as was
the desire of their grandmother/great grandmother,
Helen Boyd Camp.

This love of which I speak is slow to lose patience.
It looks for a way of being constructive.
It is not possessive.
It is neither anxious to impress nor does it cherish inflated ideas
    of its own importance.
Love has good manners and does not pursue selfish advantages.
It is not touchy.
It does not keep account of evil or gloat over the wickedness of
    other people.
On the contrary, it is glad with all good men when truth prevails!

Love knows no limit to its endurance,
No end to its trust,
No fading of its hope.
It can outlast anything!
It is, in fact, the one thing that still stands when all else has
    fallen . . . .

In this life we have three great lasting qualities: faith, hope and
    love.
But the greatest of them is love!

I Corinthians 13:4-7 plus
Phillips Translation

TABLE OF CONTENTS

The man who cannot wonder, who does not habitually wonder
and worship . . . is but a pair of spectacles, behind which there
is no Eye.

Thomas Carlyle
Sartor Resartus, Bk 1, ch 10

This book evolves from life-enriching experiences afforded as
a result of an overseas assignment; it is the unanticipated by-
product of new friendships developed, horizons and under-
standings broadened, the joys of subsequent travels and meetings.

In 1975, the first year of the International Decade of Women, I,
too, was among those wondering about the status and roles of
women in the world at large. As one of a team at Michigan State
University, I was involved in the planning and research for a series of instructional films. These were to give an overview of the
history, cultures and contributions of the peoples inhabiting ancient Persia/Iran.

I looked forward to visiting this land about which I had heard
so much: to walk some of the territory of the world's first great
empire; to see for myself the areas and artifacts relating to the
Persian kings of whom I've read in my worship. I wondered if I
would meet any People of the Book, as early Christians were
called? And I wondered how I would be received? I hoped I
would be perceived for what I am—an appreciative learner,
friendly observer and enthusiastic visitor. I wondered, too, if I'd
have the opportunity to mingle with any of modern Iran's wom-
en, in their varied ethnic/religious/socio-economic/geographic
areas?

During my stay in Iran, my hopes were more than fulfilled. In the course of my travels and interviews, I had the pleasure of meeting Iranian women from varied and contrasting walks of life. It was from them that I learned of Jane Doolittle. Their love and appreciation for this small, modest, no-nonsense, quiet-spoken American, seemed genuine and deep.

Her lifetime of selfless service in the name of Christ has ennobled the lives of the many she touched. She was beloved by the poor and needy, the children, the elderly and the ill. Among the wealthy, an admiration for her godliness prompted many to become aware of and do more for the less fortunate about them. It was her demonstration of God's unconditional love, His compassion and outreach to all, that formed the basis for her long-lasting cross-cultural friendships.

To her many friends who urged me to undertake the telling of this story, and for their generous help in so doing, I feel a deep appreciation. And to the many other dear people who have added their talent, expertise and encouragement goes my everlasting thanks.

ERRATA/OMISSIONS

I have conscientiously tried to avoid mistakes, misstatement and omissions of important detail. However, please accept my apologies for any bloopers and blights you may discover. This is not a treatise on socio-economic-political issues; rather, it is a series of related vignettes depicting imperfect humans interacting as they seek to find and give purpose and meaning to life.

TRANSLITERATION

The varied spellings/names/designations used for people and places are a cause for serious concern. In efforts to avoid misunderstanding and confusion, I selected the terminology which seemed to be most easily recognized and pronounced by the readers.

In sum, this labor of love is intended to reflect the kindness, caring and loving outreach of the many People of the Book who, past and present, demonstrate that they are respectful of others, who foster peace and goodwill toward all, who endeavor to see the world with the Eye of God, to walk in the Light as He is in the Light, to be His witnesses in the uttermost parts of the earth, and to love as He loves them.

Each of us, one by one, is part of God's human continuum. Each of us gives our own special and unique touch to our time and task. Our life's journey is short; may we live God's-best-in-us. "And whatever you do in word and deed, do all in the name of the Lord Jesus, giving thanks through Him to God the Father" (Colossians 3:17) .

Another one of the People of the Book,
Elizabeth C. Kay Voorhees

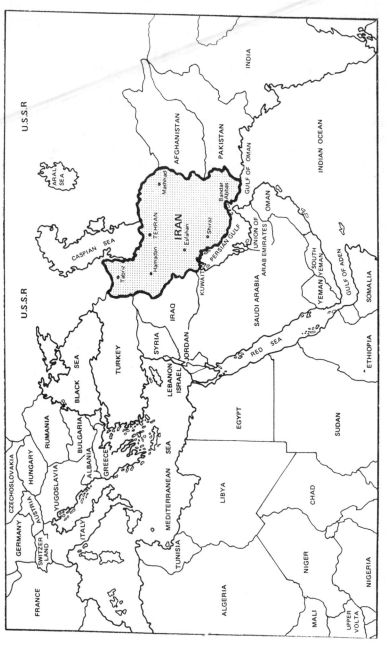

Source: Mahammed Ali Issari and Doris A. Paul, *A Picture of Persia* (Hicksville, NY, Exposition Press, 1977).

A Star in Fantasy Land

T he taxi cut skillfully into the hotel's short
semi-circular driveway. It lurched to a
pause, its motor running, in its designated space. A watchful
doorman hurried to the curb. This royal blue uniformed knight,
wearing a military-style, black-visored blue cap, hastened to
open the car door, bowing deeply to welcome the guest. The lone
occupant, a man, hopped out quickly. While his baggage was
being unloaded, the man stood impatiently on the cement walk
tapping his feet noisily. He surveyed his new surroundings
with keen interest.

The night, clear and bright, was illumined by winking stars
giving their own snappy salute. In the distance, the brilliant
white mantle of a towering, snow-capped mountain caught the
visitor's eye. Aha! Mount Damavand. "18,934 feet high, vol-
canic-coned." He was pleased to recognize what he'd just seen
pictured in his travel brochure. The hotel driveway, he noted,
was jammed bumper-to-bumper with shiny chauffeur-driven
Mercedes forming a long curving processional inching toward
the entrance where he stood.

Suddenly, a porter appeared and grabbed his baggage. The
guest, tipping his driver and the doorman, followed the porter
into the lobby. What a huge place! Crystal chandeliers, their
clusters of small lights gently swaying, brightly reflected their
dancing images in the mirrored walls and the enormous glass
windows. Tall, leafy green plants gracefully entwined the marble support pillars. Dozens of gold velour-upholstered divans
nestled upon thick deep-blue, flower-patterned carpets that
muted the sounds of moving feet. People were everywhere: sit-

1

ting, standing, walking about, laughing, chatting, sipping drinks brought by fleet-footed waiters in gold jackets.

At the registration desk, the man and his luggage were jostled and pushed by the crowd around him.

"What's going on here?" he asked.

"Pardon me, sir?" replied the clean-shaven, neatly groomed young Iranian clerk leaning toward the new guest.

"Is this a convention?" he asked, raising his voice over the noise.

"No, it's a party," the clerk replied, carefully articulating his English.

The guest eyed the elegantly clad women and their escorts, tailor-perfect in high quality European suits, as they streamed on toward the far end of the lobby. By craning his neck, he was able to read "BALLROOM" in large gold lettering.

"Please, sir," reminded the clerk, "finish registering."

"Okay, okay" replied the man checking his card. *Arya Sheraton Hotel. Tehran, Iran.* He wrote the date: *February 10, 1972.*

"Clerk!" asked the guest suddenly. "Is this a party for the Prime Minister or one of—"

"No!" interrupted the clerk. "It's just some woman . . . ."

"The queen?" hoped the visitor.

"Oh, no!" replied the annoyed clerk. "Some American."

"Who?" continued the guest, putting his pen on the counter. "I'm an American. Who is it? How can I get a reservation?"

"Sorry, it's private" the clerk snapped brusquely.

"Well, at least give me the celebrity's name. I travel constantly and know all the important people," persisted the visitor.

The clerk dangled the long, royal blue key-holder toward the porter who grasped it and then stooped to stack the man's bags. "Room 1014, sir. Follow the porter."

"Very well," replied the guest, "and the American woman's name, please?"

"Bah!" muttered the clerk. "Do—, do something; Doolittle."

The American, briefcase, topcoat and travel brochure in hand, closely followed the porter and his baggage to the closed elevator doors. "Hm", the man mused, looking back toward the crowd of excited people still parading down the hall. "Must be hundreds of them packing in there. What can they be celebrating? Who's this Doolittle person? Related to Jimmy? I've got to find out." The porter motioned to the guest and they entered the elevator amid a crush of up-goers.

After quickly freshening up, the new guest headed straight down to the ballroom.

The stage was set. Six-foot tall, white wicker baskets stood filled with brilliant crimson and pure white gladiolus. Lilting melodies from an Iranian stringed ensemble increased the sense of excitement and anticipation among the waiting guests. A technician carefully tested the audio system and adjusted the microphone.

"Pardon me, could you tell me what this is all about?" asked the curious American, addressing the reception committee standing in the ballroom doorway.

"Don't you know?" whispered a beautiful young woman. "Oh, my . . . ."

An official-looking man, holding a sheaf of papers, stepped forward, "Jane Doolittle," he said, "is the most admired American woman in the history of Iran."

"This is an anniversary for a remarkable woman," added a small, olive-skinned, gray-haired lady. "By chance are you also an American?"

"Yes, I am." He pulled out his identification card.

"Oh! United Press International. . . . A foreign correspondent?"

"Yes, always on the go." He flipped his card case shut, moving aside for a tray-laden waiter. Groups of people were clattering down a nearby marble stairway.

"We'd be honored to have you join us for this dinner. Have you time?"

"I'll make time." He bowed. "Thank you very much."

"Fine," said his hostess. "Please follow me and my granddaughter," nodding to the young woman he'd just observed, who joined them as they went downstairs. "Our dinner is being served in the hotel's largest dining hall. There are about a thousand of us here tonight," she added with a sparkling smile.

They entered a huge room, already filled with happy, noisy people who were standing together in small clusters or moving about a long curved buffet counter.

"Please take a plate from this end," suggested his hostess, "and serve yourself to whatever you like best. As you can see, most of the guests are standing as they eat. However, my granddaughter and I will be seated at that small table near the entrance so we can greet the later guests. We'll be watching for you."

A waiter, noticing the two women, hurried to the table and pulled out a chair for each. "Akbar," said the hostess, "please bring another chair for a guest who is visiting with us for the first time. And presently we'd like some of the hot hors d'oeuvres."

Meantime, the guest was filling his plate with some of the many epicurean delights. Walking carefully among the crowd, he reached the little table where the hostess awaited his arrival.

"What a sumptuous array of food! I'm so glad to be here. Thank you for inviting me," he smiled at the two as he sat down.

"You know," said his hostess, "it occurs to me you may also be interested in this book prepared for the occasion. My granddaughter and I were both students of Miss Doolittle and we helped to write this story. It commemorates her fifty years of service in our country."

"How interesting. I'd be delighted."

Scanning the pages, he noted that Jane Doolittle was from New York. "Oh, she went to Wells College?"

"Yes. You probably know that was one of the first women's colleges you had in the States."

He continued to thumb the pages. "Oh, she was on the hockey team, . . . in the drama club, . . . one of the mandolin players, . . . member of the science club, . . . president of the YWCA in her senior year, . . . delegate to the Student Volunteer Conference, in Des Moines, Iowa, in 1919 and general chairman of the conference when it came to Wells in 1921!"

"Tell me," he faced his hostess, looking intently into her

eyes, "what motivated a girl like this to come to Iran fifty years ago?"

"Oh," smiled his hostess broadly, "Miss Doolittle always has had a ready answer to that question: 'I am a servant of God. I go where He leads.'"

"Well, even so, how did she fit in with your culture in those early years?"

"Very well. Her parents and family were always important to her. Her people were of good birth and learning; always respectful and considerate. She is a modest person who doesn't like a lot of fuss and show. This celebration tonight is probably an embarrassment to her in many ways. But we, her students and admirers, offer it both as a means of expressing our love for her and as a fund-raising benefit for the Doolittle Clinic which she established to help the poor and needy."

"You must be pleased with this turnout!" Then, "could I keep this book, or get a copy? I'd like to show it to a correspondent friend of mine who is better acquainted with Iran than I."[1]

"Yes, keep it and share it with our compliments."

As he finished eating, the hostess rose and said, "Now it is time for all of us to move back upstairs to the ballroom."

Upstairs, a blazing yellow spotlight illuminated the center stage. Slightly to the left of the stage, sitting in plain sight for all her friends to see, was Jane Doolittle. The room became quiet, and all eyes focused on the stage, as the Mistress of Ceremonies walked to the microphone to introduce the guest of honor.

The drama of Jane Doolittle's life is a twentieth century Persian folktale. It began when a young, slender, brown-eyed college graduate from New York arrived in Tehran. She was a stranger, alone and uncertain. The morning was dark . . . .

NOTE

1. Referring to world traveler Herrick B. Young, the son of a Presbyterian minister, began his career in the Middle East as a United Press foreign correspondent. From 1925-1935, Dr. Young was a Professor of Literature at Alborz College in Tehran. In subsequent years he was made a Fellow of the Royal Geographic Society and of the Royal Central Asian Society. He was also decorated by the Shah of Iran in 1962.

Dr. Young's travel in Central America and the Caribbean supplemented his observations on seven trips to Latin America and prompted his writing *Hemisphere Neighbors* in 1940. Other travels took him to Africa. He wrote *Africa Seethes* about the birth of new nations and their struggle for economic independence. From 1935-1950, Dr. Young had world wide responsibility for missionary personnel under the Presbyterian Board of Foreign Missions. He directed the International House Associates, Inc., in New York, from 1950-1953 and was chairman for the Overseas Staff Committee of the International YMCA. From 1953-1969, Dr. Young served as President of Western College for Women in Oxford, Ohio. The development of a program of international education for women was a particular focus of his leadership as president. Under the United Board for Christian Higher Education in Asia, Dr. Young and his wife, Charlotte, left their home in Quaker Hill, Mt. Pleasant, Ohio, to give time in Taiwan (1969-1972) as consultant to Tunghai University. After concluding this assignment, the Youngs returned to Quaker Hill and lived there until Charlotte's death in 1982. *The Specter of World Hunger* grew out of his five years as president of the Near East Foundation. Dr. Young currently lives in New York.

Part I

Teach Me Now of Persia's Way

CHAPTER ONE

Wake Up!

What's that?"
Jane sat up in bed and strained to orient herself in the darkness of the room. "Where am I?" she wondered. "And, who is calling? It's so dark! Why would anyone be up now?"

She listened intently as the shrill, high-pitched call began again. Abruptly the intoning tapered off, and only the chirping of a few birds punctuated the early morning silence.

Jane relaxed a bit, snuggling further down under the blankets again. "Now I know where I am—I'm in Persia." The call was not for her, so she dozed off again.

Never before had she been so close to the call of the "muezzin."[1] The mosque and minaret must be nearby.

This was Jane's first journey out of America. Terrified of the seas as a child, she had once sworn she'd never cross the Atlantic. Not Jane. Her sister, Catherine, always had great plans for trips to Europe; yet, here was Jane, at age twenty-two, the first of the two to travel across the ocean. She was anxious to see and know everything about her new land. Her almost-daily travel letters home were filled with jubilant accounts of adventurous experiences. What a world! So much to learn, to see and to do.

As the morning sun flooded her room, Jane opened her eyes, blinking off her sleepiness. She gently jogged her memory again. This had to be Saturday, October, 29, 1921. "I'm in Tehran, at last—seems like years, but I'm here."

Propping up on an elbow, Jane lifted herself out of the narrow metal-springed bed. A spring noisily uncoiled itself as her bare feet hit the cold floor. Almost knocking over the kerosene lamp,

9

she hastily made for the rug.

The high ceilinged, white-walled room was unlike any she'd ever slept in before. "Here's ready for a new adventure. I'm in Persia: land of the Medes and Persians and Wisemen. Mysterious, mystical, once-mighty Persia; home of the world's first great empire, 2500 years ago."

Tingles of delight warmed her. "Heavenly Father, help me do Thy will at this time, in this place. Help me to be a good teacher to the girls . . . ."

A sudden memory flashed to mind. Just a few months ago, one of Jane's best friends at college had been in an auto accident which cut and bruised her face badly. The young woman had been expecting to teach biology to the Aurora High School seniors, but now could not. Jane was pressed into service.

Teaching at Aurora had proved to be a difficult chore. The students were completely uninterested and undisciplined. Further, Jane was not an experienced teacher. Several times, Jane had seen the principal peering through the hall window into her classroom and this had made her jumpy. But, she nonetheless had been determined to do a good job with the fifteen to twenty boys and girls unexpectedly in her care.

"Teaching here in Persia will be different," Jane reasoned. "I expect the girls attending Iran Bethel will be coming because they want to learn. Iran Bethel: The House of God."

Finding the wash water and towels on the basin stand in a closet, Jane gave her face a good healthy scrub and brushed her teeth carefully. After sliding quickly into her travel clothes, draped over the bedstead, Jane combed her soft brown hair, pinning it in place.

Even though she'd arrived in Tehran very late the night before, Jane had been warmly welcomed by the young American teachers on the staff. They, and other missionaries, had graciously shared some furnishings with her. Their thoughtfulness gave the room a homey touch. At some future date her own three-year supply of goods and furnishings would arrive, she hoped.

Not hearing any sounds outside, Jane quietly opened her bedroom door and tiptoed out. She knew in her bones it must be time for breakfast and she looked into the dining room across the hall. The dining room was only large enough for a table with four chairs. A samovar sat on a smaller table. Adjacent was the living room which she remembered from the previous evening, a rather plain, but pleasant room with a worn Persian rug and a big, old, comfortable Morris chair. A bookcase and a couple of easy chairs completed the furnishings. Through the windows she glimpsed a high mud wall running to the East and a porch leading to a lovely garden with huge trees to the South.

She thought of Charlotte Young, one of the other teachers. Charlotte seemed so warm and hospitable. Jane looked forward to being friends with her. Jane wondered where Miss Young, Miss Peet and Miss McHenry were? She ventured into the dining room.

Hearing her steps, the cook turned and came toward her with a warm smile. "Salaam," said the short, dark-complexioned, young man.

Jane wasn't sure what he had said—she'd have to get a Persian-English dictionary immediately—but she returned the smile and said, "Good morning, how are you?"

"Coffee? Tea?" he asked, pointing to the pot sitting on the samovar. He was obviously proud of his few words of English.

"Coffee, please," Jane replied.

The cook motioned for Jane to be seated at the small table set with a brownish cloth stamped with some kind of leaf pattern. A serving plate, silverware and a small bouquet of orange chrysanthemums graced the table. "Nice." Jane saw a folded piece of paper at her place; she picked it up and looked at the cook. He nodded and smiled encouragingly. "'Baleh'(yes)! 'Khanum' (madame) Peet for you."

The hastily scrawled note read: "Sorry, forgot to say breakfast is at 7:00 A.M. Coming for you at 8:30 A.M. Armenian cook's name, Sahok, he'll help you. G.P."

"Sahok?" asked Jane, trying out the new word. She looked up and they both smiled.

"Sahok, your humble servant." He bowed again, then went off to get her toast and eggs.

Jane opened the small, black, leather-bound New Testament/ Psalms edition she always carried instead of the heavy Bible her father had given to each of his children in turn. Following his example, she read her daily chapter, then bowed her head in prayerful thanksgiving to her loving Heavenly Father for her earthly father, mother and family. She asked God's blessing on all their needs; and that He would bless her work here, as well as all who were laboring in Christ's name.

She breakfasted hastily, realizing it was nearly 8:30.

She was eager to get on with her short-term assignment here. Her long-held objective was to obtain a medical degree and serve as a physician in Africa. However, as an introduction to foreign service, she'd agreed to come to Iran Bethel, the American Presbyterian school for girls founded in Tehran in 1874.

In her junior year at Wells, Jane had gone as a delegate to the Student Volunteer Conference in Des Moines, Iowa (December, 1919).[2] The theme of the conference had been the challenge to "Evangelize the World in This Generation," and Jane had accepted the challenge, signing a pledge purposing to become a missionary.

Later, Dr. William McElwee Miller,[3] a young Princeton seminarian in Persia, had challenged the Wells' students to send a graduate to teach at the Iran Bethel school in Tehran. The students accepted the challenge, and soon raised the required $3,000 support money. However, a greater problem remained: there was no one willing to go. Few of them knew much about Persia; and parents were not eager to see their daughters sent off into an unsettled country.

As president of the Wells' YWCA, Jane gave her enthusiastic leadership to the Persian project, all the while carrying on with her demanding pre-med studies (Chemistry, Physics, Biology, etc.). The medical schools at both Cornell and Columbia University had already accepted her application for admission. She was steadily advancing toward her goal of becoming a physician, intent on going to Africa. Her only question was which school to go to next year?

However, Jane's classmates knew she'd previously signed that Student Volunteer pledge to become a foreign missionary. They began to wonder about her commitment. She began to wonder, too. What was she willing to do? What was her goal? Geography? People? Profession? God? Finally, after much soul-searching and prayer, Jane decided to accept this short-term (three-year) challenge.[4]

Though her parents believed Jane was too young to go so far beyond their reach, they became supportive when they saw that Jane's commitment was firm. So, within weeks of graduation from college (June, 1921), Jane was standing on the deck of the "SS City of York" (August 17), excitedly waving farewell to her beloved family and saying a breezy "au 'voir" to the Statue of Liberty.

Usually, travelers to Persia made the trip via Russia. However, because of the political unrest there after the Communist revolution, Jane and her companions were routed through India. The steamship plowed the rough waters all the way to Bombay with only a brief stop for refueling at Port Said in Egypt. Here, Jane, and some of the other thirty missionaries on board, bound for India or the Middle East, went ashore for two days, visiting Cairo and the sphinx at Memphis. Thirty-two days was a long time to be on board ship, especially for Jane who had always been fearful of ocean travel.

On reaching Bombay, however, her concern was how to get to Tehran. Ghandi's India was in socio-political upheaval and, consequently, there wasn't much transportation available for anyone. While thus unexpectedly delayed in India, Jane and three other young missionaries took a train to Allahabad and Aqra. As much as they could, they experienced the fascinating sights, sounds, smells and culture of a society very unlike their own.

On their return to the ship, they received word that transportation would be available for three people only on the very next day. Fifteen or sixteen missionaries were heading for Persia, but they decided that Jane should be one of those to go ahead, since the school where she was to teach was already in session. She was badly needed in Tehran.

The next morning, Jane and a newlywed couple, along with three other passengers, set sail for a week's journey on a ship coursing the Persian Gulf to Busra, Mesopotamia (now in Iraq). Arriving at Busra, the missionaries arranged their transportation to Baghdad via the British-built, narrow gauge railway.

Jane was thrilled to be in the ancient city of Baghdad. Visions of the "Thousand and One Nights", of "Ali Baba and the Forty Thieves", and all the other exotic tales she'd read as a child came bubbling to mind. Jane also remembered stories of another era and culture; real events that took place long before the fantasies were dreamed up. About 1800 B.C., God had spoken to a man named Abraham who lived in a city called Ur, on the Euphrates River some miles south of where Jane was now standing. Maybe his journey of faith had brought Abraham and his family and flocks near this very place.

However, instead of Abraham's tents, Jane saw a sea of refugee tents surrounding the unfinished YMCA building. Caught up in World War I conflicts and seeking safety from further persecutions at the hands of their enemies, the Turks, these Assyrian refugees had recently escaped from Urumia, their age-old settlement in northwest Persia. Dr. Philip McDowell, a medical missionary to Persia, temporarily assigned to Baghdad to oversee the plight of the thousands escaping the massacres in northern Persia, showed the visitors around.

The McDowells were living in a section of the unfinished "Y" building and offered Jane and her companions hospitality. After showing the newlyweds, Merrel and Eleanor Marker, to a comfortable room, Dr. McDowell took Jane to a bare room containing only a bed. However, Jane was thankful for the bed and was soon sound asleep.

During the night Jane was suddenly awakened when a nightshirted Dr. McDowell hurried into the room to see if Jane were frightened. There was an eclipse of the moon and hundreds of the city's residents were lined up along the Tigris River. They were shrieking, wailing and beating drums, trying to drive off the eclipse and its evil spirits. Exhausted, Jane had not heard all the commotion. She would never have known of the event had she not been purposefully awakened by her concerned new friend.

A week later, with vivid memories of Baghdad, Jane and the Markers bid farewell to the McDowells and boarded the narrow gauge train for Rail Head, the border between Mesopotamia and Persia. The train also carried a group from the British Bank in Persia. After an all-night ride, the travelers arrived at the border. Everyone had to get off and find some other means of transportation to their destination.

Disconcertingly, the border station stood in solitary abandon in the midst of the desert. It had neither a restaurant nor a hotel.

It also did not have a predictable schedule for the arrival of other transportation. In those days, people expecting to settle in a foreign country for a while knew they needed to bring whatever supplies they would require for the journey and their length of stay. Accordingly, the British travelers had a large quantity of supplies, besides their servants and food provision. However, the young missionaries were carrying only the most needed items for their present and personal needs; beds, bedding, mosquito nets, soap and towels. Jane and her companions had very little food, but they managed.

That night, everyone spread a bed out on the desert, crawled under a mosquito net and went to sleep as best they could. Jackals wailed loudly in the distance. As Jane looked into the millions of stars overhead, it seemed that God was speaking directly to her:

The heavens declare the glory of God; and the firmament showeth His handiwork (Psalm 19:1).

She answered with a hymn: "I need Thee, oh, I need Thee. Every hour I need Thee."

He replied:

"Be strong and of good courage; I will not leave or forsake thee. Only be strong and very courageous" (Joshua 1:6, 5, 7).

"Peace I leave with you, my peace I give unto you. Let not your heart be troubled, neither let it be afraid" (John 14:27).

A comforting quietness pervaded Jane. She relaxed in the assurance of God's care even as she heard the moaning of the jackals.

Before dawn the next morning, a low, steady hum broke the stillness. Everyone rose up to listen. It was a motor. A car was coming! The British, all agog, were certain it was for them. The roar of the motor intensified; finally, in a cloud of dust, a car stopped nearby. A small, dark-skinned man bounced out and came toward the waiting group. Courteously, in heavily accented English, he said, "Mr. and Mrs. Marker, Miss Doolittle, I come for you!" He bowed.

Within an amazingly short time, the driver and the young people piled the bulky baggage on the top of the car and on the running boards, tying them securely with rope. Just past dawn,

with a friendly, "Cheeri-o and God bless" to the Britishers, the
happy missionaries climbed into the cramped car to commence
another leg of their long journey.

The trip proceeded slowly. The roadway was dry, dusty and
frequently ridged. And, as soon as their car appeared at every
little oasis or village, an official guard would appear from some-
where to lower a barrier across the path, forcing them to stop.

"Passports and credentials, please." As curious villagers
stared at the foreign strangers, the guard, as authorized, looked
at the documents in detail. Many times the driver had to assist
the usually illiterate guards as they dutifully tried to record
whatever was required. Meanwhile, clusters of dirty, ragged
little boys pushed in among the travelers hoping for a handout.

Just before nightfall, the travel-weary missionaries were
stopped at still another village at the base of a mountain pass.
Using a few words of English, a few in French, some sign language, and with a lot of Persian advice from the assembled villagers, the missionaries realized they were being told to stop in
that village for the night. "Too many bandits. Too dangerous at
night."

However, the naive newcomers, not really understanding the
language, the implications and wild gesticulations, made it clear
that they intended to continue their journey. They were already
long overdue at Kermanshah. Off they went, determined to reach
their destination. As it became darker, the driver stopped and
tied a kerosene lantern onto the front of the car for a headlight.
Every few slow, black miles, he would get out to see if he and the
road were in proximity; by the light of a match, he would make
his decision!

Years later, when Jane had occasion to travel the Zagros
mountain pass in daylight, she realized with horror the very real
dangers about which the knowledgeable villagers had tried to
warn them. Jane could only marvel at God's protective care and
remember His promise:

> "There shall no evil befall thee for He shall give His angels
> charge over thee to keep thee in all thy ways" (Psalm 91:10-11).

It was after ten o'clock that night before they found the mission compound at Kermanshah. Peering out of the car windows,

Jane and her companions could see nothing but ten-foot-high mud walls on either side of the road. When they finally pulled up at the mission gate, the driver got out and negotiated with the guard who unfastened the padlock and swung open the heavy wood and iron gate. Despite all the bulging baggage, the gate was wide enough to admit the car inside the safety of the walled mission compound.

Everything was dark. The mission personnel, knowing that nobody ever crossed the mountain pass at night, had long ago given up on the travelers. As the guard dragged the gate shut and clicked the padlock, the dogs awoke.[5] Soon, their yapping, barking and loud yelping had the missionary hosts roused and out to greet the exhausted travelers. Cordially welcomed into the adobe mission house, they were given hot soup and time to relax while their dinner was reheated. Though their prayers that night were short, their gratitude to God was profound.

Jane and her companions remained in Kermanshah for two days, resting and getting acquainted with that part of Persia. They visited the mission hospital and the dormitory built for the children who'd been orphaned in the Urumia massacre. Since automobiles were still a rarity in Persia, the resident missionaries walked or used a horse-drawn carriage. Sometimes they rode donkeys or horses. Although Jane had followed the advice of the mission's three-year list of necessities and brought riding clothes, up to now she'd never ridden a horse.

However, the next afternoon she put on her riding clothes. With a bright smile she joined her two companions for the four-mile ride to Taq-i-Bustan to see the famous bas relief carved high on the mountainside. These rock carvings date back to the time of the Sassanian kings, about A.D. 224-651. Jane looked forward to learning the history of the victories conveyed in these narrative murals. At present, however, she pondered the fact that, pictured in one of the stone carvings, a Sassanian king out on his imperial boar hunt was accompanied by groups of female musicians who were serenading him. Perhaps her mandolin would come in handy?

The next day Jane was relieved and surprised to discover that her eight-mile horseback ride had not left her with sore muscles. What a great sport, she thought. Soon it was time to pack up once again and move along toward Tehran. After prayers and happy encouragements from the resident missionaries, Jane and the Markers journeyed on to their next stop, Hamadan.

Mile after mile of dust and desert was broken only occasionally by an oasis. The travelers were glad for the small tea houses they found in these spots. While the women were not allowed to enter, for the men there was usually a "qalian hubble-bubble,"[6] along with tea, flat bread and white cheese. The driver brought some of these refreshments to the women. They wished that someone had thought of closed restrooms for their use, rather than the primitive outdoor toilets situated behind the tea house.[7]

At last they reached Hamadan—the Markers' destination. Although thrilled at finally arriving, they hated to part company from Jane. All their lives they would share the precious, frightening and humorous memories of their first journey into Persia.

Jane's journey to Tehran was continued in company with a Russian family in a car hired by the mission. They could communicate with each other only in sign language. After another long day, they arrived at Qazvin. The Russian family had business here. They took Jane to the Grand Hotel where she stayed while they went about their affairs. And it was here that she again experienced the kindness and concern of Persia's people. A servant in the hotel, an old man, tried to teach her some words he knew would be useful. "Ab-e-garm," hot water, were her first Persian words. Alone, in a strange country whose language she did not understand, she was grateful for this friendly gesture. Indeed, Jane was afraid to leave the hotel for fear of not finding it again. However, eventually she got up enough courage to walk outside a few times.

Her hotel room, like all the others, opened onto a common veranda which encircled the building. That first night, she heard noises outside her window and was sure someone was trying to enter her room. She slept very little the rest of that night. The following evening, she barricaded the door from inside and slept more comfortably. The next morning Jane and the Russian family continued on to Tehran where they parted company.

It was Friday evening, October 28, when Jane finally reached her destination in Tehran. By the time the driver successfully located the American Presbyterian compound, it was totally dark.

At first it seemed as if no one were there, but Jane's heart quickened with joy when she saw light streaming through the stained-glass windows of a church. She heard the strains of a familiar hymn, "What a friend we have in Jesus . . . ," and a lump rose in her throat. How thrilling to have, at last, arrived at her new world and work for Christ.

The driver proceeded around behind the church and stopped beside a big gate which opened into a secluded garden. Three or four people with kerosene lanterns in hand came running out toward the car. Jane jumped out, rejoicing to see young women also in their twenties.

"Welcome, welcome, Jane Doolittle! Praise the Lord, you're safely here!" Instantly, Jane was enveloped in a circle of love that would bring her companionship and treasured friends. These strong bonds of Christian fellowship and service would bless her whole life. Meanwhile, the driver unloaded her baggage and lugged it into the residence hallway. After making sure that everything of hers was accounted for, Jane laboriously counted out the driver's tip of silver coins.[8] Bowing and smiling, the driver disappeared into the darkness and Jane turned to the women waiting around her.

"I'm Gertrude Peet. I've been here the longest—four years."

"And I'm Lillian McHenry . . . ."

"Charlotte Young is my name," interrupted a petite, vivacious woman. "Lillian and I came over together. We've been here about . . . uh . . . ."

"Seven months, isn't it?" figured Lillian.

"Anyway," continued Charlotte as they moved along the pathway, "come on. We're glad you're here. How long since you left home?"

"Two months!" replied Jane.

"Two months is a long time, even to get from New York to Tehran," mused Charlotte, "but we had problems, too. We got stuck in England in January—it was bleak, damp and miserable. Then, a month later, we got stuck in Bombay. Because of political tensions with Persia, the British wouldn't give us any protection as we came up the Persian Gulf. It was really very discouraging, but we kept on believing that 'All things work together for good. . . .' It's good we can be sure of that. Now, let's get busy and help Miss Doolittle settle in."

"That'll be fine," said Jane gratefully. "How nice if I could have a good old American bath."

"Oh, no!" said Lillian in quick alarm. "Oh, Miss Doolittle," she continued apologetically, "we do not have bathtubs. No running water, no plumbing, no central heating, no electricity, phones, trains or buses."

"But you'll adjust," said Charlotte reassuringly.

They were approaching a two-storied, flat-roofed building. Miss Peet explained: "This was originally built as a dormitory and classroom area for students,[9] but Iran Bethel now uses it to house the single teachers for the school.

"And here," exclaimed Charlotte as the four of them trooped along toward the doorway, "is where we live."

"Ingleside," announced Lillian.

She opened the door and the young women walked into a small living room. Jane looked around, curious and excited. This was to be her home for the next three years. Would it be like home to her? There were some chairs, a rather worn rug and some small coffee tables. A large kerosene lantern on a center table flickered as a breeze blew in through the door which Miss Peet closed after them. The young women set their smaller lanterns in various places around the room. Jane dropped her coat and hat on a chair and sank down into the welcome soft sturdiness of an all-embracing Morris chair. "How comfortable. How good it is to be home!"

"We have some hot soup and a little food here that we've prepared for you," said Miss Peet. "Will you excuse me while I get it for you?" She took her lantern in hand and walked carefully so as not to stumble over the array of baggage that the driver had hauled in. She went outside toward the adjoining kitchen.

"Is it hard learning to speak Persian?" Jane asked.

Charlotte spoke up first: "Well, I suppose that depends on a lot of things. Persian doesn't bear much resemblance to the languages that most of us studied—Latin, French, Spanish, German, whatever. The pronounciations aren't so difficult, except for a few guttural sounds which are non existent in English. The grammar is simple, and thus not too hard to learn. But reading and writing the Arabic script is very hard! The Board gives us three years to become fluent. Unless one knows the native tongue well, there can be no real communication. Learning it is a must for new missionaries, and we all work hard on it."

Lillian agreed emphatically with Charlotte, then excused herself, lantern in hand, to help Miss Peet bring refreshments from the distant kitchen. Jane was grateful for the tea, bread and cheese which they brought.

"Please excuse me now," said Miss Peet. "I have to go prepare for tomorrow. Lillian and Charlotte will show you to your room on the ground floor." She was hoping Jane would not be nervous. "We are in the three bedrooms on the second floor. We have an outside toilet arrangement up on the porch under the roof. Charlotte will show you the ground floor accommodation which is on the way to the kitchen."

Jane started to rise out of her chair to say her thanks and good night, but Miss Peet insisted: "No, no, Miss Doolittle. Please stay where you are and be comfortable. We're glad to have you here and are looking forward to sharing our life with you. See you in the morning?"

Jane nodded and settled back down in the chair. "Thank you. I'm sure everything will be fine."

"Good night, Miss Doolittle. Charlotte, thanks for looking after our new teacher."

Miss Peet went out carrying her lantern. Jane sipped the hot tea with relish. "Please join me, Miss Young and Miss McHenry.10 Miss Peet put extra cups and food on the tray; do share with me."

Charlotte poured tea for herself, tore off a piece of the flat, crusty bread and took some of the white cheese and a few greens from the tray. "I hope you'll like Persian food," she said. "We've come to like it a lot, though it's quite different from our food in the States."

The young women chatted on happily as they ate. Jane mentioned something about late night snacks on shipboard.

"Oh, my," groaned Charlotte, remembering some of her experiences. "I boldly announced to everyone that I was not going to succumb to 'mal de mer,' and guess who wanted to die first? What a disease!" They smiled and shared in soft laughter.

"But there were good times, too," added Charlotte. "Sometimes at night members of the ship's crew would join us for entertainment. One of the men strung up my mandolin and —"

"Mandolin!" exclaimed Jane. "Do you play it, too?"

Charlotte nodded enthusiastically. "Oh yes, I love it."

They continued to discuss their varied interests and how these could be used in the school. "Have you had teaching experience?" inquired Jane.

"Oh, yes," said Charlotte. "I taught down south in Mississippi at the Mary Holmes Seminary, a Presbyterian school for Negro girls."

"How was it?" wondered Jane.

"Oh, fine! The students were giggly and shy, sort of uncertain at first, but we got along fine and had many good times. The girls loved singing, and music is one of my special delights."

"How come you're here?" asked Jane.

"Well, I'm a preacher's kid", explained Charlotte. "Are you?"

"No, my father is a chemical engineer, but my grandfather was a Congregational minister in Chester, Connecticut, so I guess that serving the Lord is just part of my heritage," Jane said.

"Well," continued Charlotte, "my father always wanted to be a foreign missionary—Siam (Thailand) was his dream. But there were too many little children in our family, and the mission board didn't want to risk sending father out. So, I guess I got the bug from him. When I applied to the board for overseas duty and was finally accepted and assigned to Persia, I was excited and happy, though somewhat apprehensive because of all the unrest in this country."

Jane briefly explained how she came to be in Persia on this short term assignment, instead of preparing to be a missionary doctor in Africa. Then the young women arose, collecting some of the baggage to take to Jane's room. As Lillian extinguished one lamp, Charlotte picked up hers and escorted Jane to her new room. She lit the kerosene lamp there for Jane and started to show her about the room.

However, Jane barely heard all of Charlotte's, "Here's the . . . and here's this . . . and over there . . . and under that . . . for your bag." She ended with, "The lamp turns off here; more blankets are over there. God give you rest and peace and joy. We're glad you're here and we'll see you in the morning. By the way, my room is just to the left at the top of the stairs."

Charlotte took her lantern and started out of the room. "Sweet dreams," she whispered as she quietly shut the door.

Wearily fighting off an enveloping sense of loneliness and let-down, Jane made herself ready for rest. Turning off the lantern with conscious care, she sank into the narrow cold bed. "The blackness of night is so dense when one is alone, tired and in an unfamiliar place," she thought.

Hours later, Jane stirred. "I'm cold." She forced her eyelids to open a bit. "Where are the extra blankets?" but she still couldn't see a thing. Buried in total darkness, she dozed off again.

"That voice! Who's calling?" Jane roused herself to listen. It was the muezzin calling the faithful to prayers. His voice seemed close, then far, and, finally, it faded out altogether.

NOTES

1. A "muezzin" is the man who calls Muslims to prayer five times a day.

2. The Student Volunteer Movement, one of the most influential missionary movements in history, celebrated its centennial in 1986. In 1886, at a summer Bible school conference in Mt. Hermon, Massachusetts, sponsored by Dwight L. Moody and the Young Men's Christian Association (YMCA), 100 young college men decided to become foreign missionaries. One of the "Mt. Hermon 100" was John R. Mott, an officer of the Cornell University YMCA. Thereafter throughout his lifetime, he promoted the watchword "The Evangelization of the World in This Generation." He interpreted this to mean " . . . give all men an adequate opportunity to know Jesus Christ as their Savior and to become His real disciples." Each generation, he said, must evangelize itself. (As cited by Dana L. Robert in The International Bulletin of Missionary Research, Vol. 10, No. 4, October, 1986.) Cornell University and Wells College are within a few miles of each other. By the time Jane Doolittle was a student at Wells, many colleges had chapters of the Student Volunteer Organization. Jane was president of the New York State group.

3. Dr. Miller became one of the most dedicated and influential Presbyterian missionaries in Persia, serving there between 1919 and 1960. He is the author of many books.

4. Jane was the first graduate of Wells College to go to Persia on an educational mission to the Iran Bethel School for Girls. Her initial sup-

port was raised by the Wells students themselves. At that time, $3,000 took care of all the basic essentials (travel, housing, food, etc.) for one year. Later, Jane's support was provided by a series of churches, including her own church in Yonkers, New York, one in Cranbury, New Jersey and one near Harrisburg, Pennsylvania. Wells College also supported other Wells women in Iran. Winifred Pomeroy taught for three years at Iran Bethel. Then Helen Rose taught for one year. Charlotte Stone took Helen's place and later married a distinguished Persian gentleman, remaining in Iran for many years. In 1929, Margaret Brown was the last of the Wells' graduates to be supported. She subsequently married Jim Hill, one of the other teachers at Alborz College.

5. Persians, in general, were not fond of dogs and did not keep them as household pets.

6. A "qalian hubble-bubble" is a quart-sized bottle of water with a pipe attached. The water prevents the smoker from inhaling the drug through the pipe.

7. The outdoor toilets were enclosed by mud walls. At the entrance was always an "aftabeh," the watering can used in Persia in place of toilet paper.

8. Printed money was only good when used in the city where it was printed. Therefore, travelers had to carry silver money, usually in big muslin bags.

9. When Iran Bethel was founded, in 1874, it was a boarding school.

10. People did not immediately use another's first name in those days.

CHAPTER TWO

Across Cultures

C offee?"
        Jane's reveries of the previous night
were interrupted as Sahok quietly returned to the dining room,
jolting Jane back to the present and her first breakfast in Tehran.

"Coffee?" repeated Sahok more softly.

"No, thank you. I am fine." The cook left as silently as he had
come.

Jane realized she'd had a restless night and that she was still
restless. The call of the muezzin had disturbed her sleep. When
would it come again? Yet a sense of peace filled her with hope as
she contemplated the joy of making friends with people who
worshipped their god so faithfully. "Early in the morning I will
praise Thy name, O Lord."

The door opened. "Good morning, Miss Doolittle," said Gertrude Peet coming in. "A principal always hopes her teachers
will be on time. I'm glad you are. Sorry that I've kept you waiting. Did Sahok bring everything you wanted?"

Jane nodded. "Yes. Breakfast was very nice."

"Did you sleep well last night? Your first night may have
seemed rather strange."

"It was fine, thank you. I'm eager to know more about my
work."

"Good! We appreciate dedication and enthusiasm," said Miss
Peet. "Charlotte and Lillian are already in their language classes;
they have rather heavy schedules. Yesterday, being Friday, was
the Muslim holy day. Today, I'm going to show you around the
school, and tomorrow you'll have more time to get oriented and
to plan. Every Sunday morning we all attend a church service

25

given in the Persian language. We also have a daily program of worship and song in our school. Every Monday at five the missionaries get together for prayer and business in one of the missionary homes. This Monday you will begin your teaching. How does that sound?" asked Miss Peet.

Jane took a big breath, nodded and smiled. "Fine! But I'm anxious to know more about the school."

"Of course." Then Miss Peet gave her a brief overview. When Iran Bethel was founded in 1874 by the American Presbyterians, the students were all Armenians. At that time, Muslim girls did not go to school since educating women wasn't considered important or worthwhile, although the "mullahs" (the Muslim clergymen) sometimes went to private homes to teach the women and girls to read certain passages of the Quran. Because of this tradition, it wasn't until 1915 that the school had its first Muslim graduates. But as the years passed, many girls from the most respected Muslim families attended Iran Bethel in search of education.

In the beginning, not many of the Persian students were very serious about education. Early marriages were arranged for them and if for some reason they didn't care to continue at school, dropping out was a simple matter. Also, in the earliest years of the school students boarded year-round.

"However," concluded Miss Peet, "we are no longer in that boarding program. We are now a day school only. We have excellent rapport with the parents, and a wonderful group of students. I can tell you more about them later; let me show you the facilities first."

"I can hardly wait to begin," exclaimed Jane.

Miss Peet took her on a complete tour of the building and classes. The American mission had three compounds and, with few exceptions, all of the missionary personnel in Tehran, regardless of function and assignment, lived on mission property. The central compound, where Jane lived and worked, was the location not only of the girls' school, but also of a boys' school and the church sanctuary. There were also two residences and some servants' quarters.

A mile northwest of the central compound there was some property purchased for the future men's college. This would expand the current educational program for boys, and the two missionary families currently involved in the boys' work lived there. Two miles northeast of the central compound was the American Mission Hospital. This facility and its staff were among the most highly respected in all of the country.[1] There were also two residences on this property.

The girls' school in the central compound had been originally built for a dormitory while the eastern section was used for living quarters for the single women missionaries. This was Ingleside where Jane now lived with the three other young women.

As the weekend passed, Jane learned more and more about Iran Bethel and became increasingly eager to begin teaching. Then, at last, it was Monday.

She read her Bible and prayed, then dressed hurriedly. Promptly at 7 A.M. Jane appeared for breakfast. Afterwards she shared in the morning devotions with her housemates. The devotions marked the beginning of her learning the Persian language.

Soon she would enter a classroom and face her girls. What would they be like? Would their fathers, like hers, expect their daughters to do their best?

As she entered the classroom, walking briskly with poise and purpose, the waiting girls quickly rose and stood at respectful attention. This was their English class.

"Good morning, girls." Jane spoke enthusiastically but quietly. Her brown eyes were alive with curiosity and a friendly smile warmed her face.

"Good morning!" exclaimed the girls in unison. They wanted to say more, but were afraid, being unsure of the proper words.

"Please be seated," instructed Jane.

Noiselessly, the girls quickly sat at their desks. They lowered their heads, glancing furtively from one to another, to teacher and back. They had known for months that they'd be getting a new teacher. They were anxious to discover what this young American was all about. They would test her out as soon as they could.

In looking at them, Jane remembered vividly just what life was like for her at this age. Since she had been frail as a child, the rigors of getting to and from public school in Yonkers, New

York, were often too taxing. Many times the family doctor had not permitted her to go to school. But her mother, Grace Ferguson Doolittle, had also been frail as a child and had taught Jane to use her active, inquiring mind.

By the time Jane was ten, she'd read everything she could find: Dickens, Scott, the old Muhlbach historical novels and the classics. It was the story of *Mary Slessor of Calabar*, the young Scottish missionary to Africa, which profoundly affected Jane's lifetime decisions.[2]

As she now faced her class, Jane plunged into the subject at hand, not fully realizing how little English the girls really understood. In time Jane would see her mistake and adjust her teaching accordingly.

After classes, Jane returned to Ingleside. Ingleside was taking a little getting used to. For one thing, Jane's genteel background had not given her much experience in dealing with ways unlike her own. And there were many new customs to learn. The residence had a small dining room and an outside kitchen in back of the building, but no bathroom. Upstairs there was a toilet in a shed out on the roof, and one downstairs on the way to the kitchen. Using the upstairs facility in winter was a chilling experience, while the one downstairs offered little privacy. Furthermore, there were other complications: these were not flush toilets, just an opening in the ground, over which foreigners, not used to squatting, placed a wooden seat.[3] All of this was new to Jane.

Another new practice for Jane concerned bathing. She smiled as she remembered the old saying, "I can't take a bath, it's not Saturday." Evidently, that was literally true at Ingleside. An old galvanized tub was carried from one bedroom to another for a weekly bath. A servant would bring in two buckets of water, one hot, one cold. It wasn't too difficult to pour the water from the buckets into the tub, but it was quite a chore after bathing to empty the water from the tub back into the buckets. In winter they pulled the tub into the downstairs living room where an open fire provided needed heat.

The American custom of sitting in a bathtub after scrubbing seemed very crude and unclean to the Persians. Most used the public baths where clientele of the same sex bathed together. Every district had at least one public bath that was used by men and women at different hours. Some districts had separate facilities. The bathing ritual was often a day-long affair, especially for the women. This was the place where older women had the opportunity to view and judge prospective brides for their male relatives. The women would soak, get scrubbed by the attendant, relax, visit and gossip. At noon a servant would bring a good lunch. Most Persian women bathed every two weeks or once a month (as circumstances allowed).[4]

Since no water was piped into the homes, a waterman delivered fresh water to the kitchen every morning. The American's fresh water came from the British Embassy's protected "qanat", or aqueduct, which brought water underground from the nearby mountains. The waterman emptied this water into a galvanized drum from a goat's skin container hung over his back. Every drop of this water was purchased, and was used only for drinking and cooking.

The water used for bathing, cleaning clothes, and for irrigating the garden, was brought to homes through open street gutters, called "jubes". This water was stored in a reservoir or underground tank and arrived every two or three weeks in the middle of the night. There would be a loud knocking on the garden gate and the "mir-ab" (waterman) would come in, carrying a lantern and a shovel, to direct the water from the jubes into the reservoir and irrigation channels. This water, of course, was not fit to drink. All households had a central pool in the middle of their enclosed garden.

Some food staples, such as rice and onions, were also delivered to the house. These arrived in huge bags borne by a donkey to the kitchen door. They were weighed and poured into the buyer's containers. Other foodstuffs, however, had to be obtained in the marketplace. Each day the cook went to the food shops to haggle over every little item. Sahok had to give a daily accounting to the missionaries for the products he purchased; not an easy task since he could neither read nor write and had to rely on his memory. Also, as was the custom, the servant added a small percentage to each item purchased as fee for service.

Of course, electricity was practically non-existent in Persia in 1921. Jane soon discovered the kerosene lamps must be moved carefully or they would go out. And, cooking on charcoal or wood was also different from the American gas stoves to which she was accustomed.

Telephones were a rarity and most communication was delivered by a servant. Frequently the answer to a note would be written on the back of its envelope. Eventually the gatekeeper at the central compound had a telephone; he received all incoming calls and sent a messenger to locate the person being called.

Early on, Jane noticed that her home country and her new country viewed time very differently. Persians considered time more casually than Americans. The teachers often found it difficult to get the girls to class at the scheduled hour. If one were invited to a meal, no definite hour would be set. "Come around 11:00" or "come at 5:00" was the usual invitation, but that did not mean that luncheon was served at 11:00 or dinner at 5:00. Many times the teachers would arrive at a home at the specified hour only to discover that they would be served refreshments for two hours or more while the other guests continued to saunter in. Sometimes the evening meal would not be served until after 10:30 P.M., even though the invitation had been for 5:00 P.M. or 6:00 P.M. With this arrangement, as soon as the meal was finished after another serving of tea, the guests were expected to leave.

Another difference about time arose because, for a Persian, a day began at sundown. When a Persian said, "Wednesday eve", he meant Tuesday night by American reckoning. Once, before Jane and the others understood this practice, they were caught in an embarrassing situation. They had been invited to dinner on "Saturday eve" at the home of a recently married graduate. Since Friday is the day of worship and a holiday in Iran, the teachers were out on a picnic until after 7:00 P.M. When they returned to Ingleside, they were surprised to find a messenger from their hostess wondering why Jane and the other guests had not yet arrived for dinner. The young women hurriedly changed their clothes and dashed to Heshmat's home which, fortunately, was nearby. On arriving they were relieved to learn that they were not unduly late as the meal was not to be served until after 10:00 P.M. Thereafter, Jane was very careful to check any invitations as to the day.

The Iran Bethel teachers were expected to call in the homes of their students, and each afternoon the teachers would make a visit to someone's home. It was traveling through the streets of Tehran making these visits that Jane felt the greatest differences between her American culture and that of the Persians. Then a small city with a population of about 200,000, Tehran was completely surrounded by high walls that had twelve gates and a moat encircling the walls.[5] The city was small enough that people could usually walk wherever they were going. But, when necessary, they could also take a "doroshgeh"—an open carriage drawn by two horses which cost two rials (about two cents) to use.

Often, very few people would be out on the streets, and most there would be men. Once in a while Jane would observe a poor woman squatting by the roadside jube shrouded in her "chador", the all-enveloping cloth, about eight-yards in length, which completely concealed her body from head to foot. Wealthier women wore black silk chadors with an eight-inch mat of woven horsehair screening their eyes and face from the public—no part of the woman's body was to be seen. Women often walked on one side of the street and the men on the other.

Lalezar was the Fifth Avenue of Tehran, and then boasted of a horse-drawn trolley car. Window-shopping for antiques, jewelry, rugs and crafts was always an exciting adventure. Every once in a while Jane and Charlotte, who had fast become best friends, would treat themselves to the wonder of the bazaar. The bazaar was more than a market-place; it was the town square, city hall and village square all rolled into one. Many "bazaari", as the merchants were called, were involved in large financial transactions. Consequently, their unofficial power and decisions had great impact, both in Tehran and in other parts of the world. As devout Muslims, many of the bazaari supported the conservative "mullahs" (religious leaders) and were generally strongly opposed to modernization efforts within Iran.

For Jane and Charlotte the main concern in the bazaar was learning how to bargain and negotiate with the small shopkeepers. Even the purchase of a few pistachios was fun. Sometimes they'd meet one of the other thirty or so Americans who lived in Tehran, and talk together about store items that intrigued them.

A few of the shopkeepers understood a bit of English and lively attempts at conversation would often ensue.

Being a newcomer and a foreigner, Jane was eager to learn details of all the Persian customs. One friend advised, "Hospitality is an art form in this country and you will find Persians to be very gracious. Be careful that you don't praise some object in the home too much, for your host will feel obligated to give it to you on the principle that 'the guest is beloved of God.' Likewise, if you do or say something out of place, don't expect a Persian to correct you because it is considered ill-mannered to do so: 'the guest can do no wrong.'" Another advisor counseled that "when you are seated, it is considered polite for women to rise when another person of equal or higher status enters the room. And you, as a young woman, should always rise when an older man or woman enters the room, and then wait to be seated until he or she is seated."

There were many other thoughtful customs which Jane enjoyed from the very beginning. This was true of tea. As soon as a guest arrived, hot, strong tea would be promptly served by the "kolfat" (woman servant) or "nokar" (man servant). It would be served in delicate, small glasses, frequently gold-rimmed and often without handles. Rather than putting sugar pieces6 into the tea glass, Persians put the pieces into their mouths, swizzling the tea through the sugar. To be polite, a guest always sipped some of the tea. Nuts, cakes, candies and fruits were also usually served.

During those first years, Jane constantly depended on her Persian-English dictionary, finding it especially important when it was her turn to give orders to the cook. Charlotte had once inadvertently told Sahok to cut up his sister ("khahar") for lunch when she had meant to request cucumbers ("khiar").

Since Africa had been Jane's planned mission destination, she had not studied much Persian history at home. However, she did know that Persia is first mentioned in the Bible in 2 Chronicles 36:22-23, which recounted the decree of Cyrus, king of Persia, for rebuilding the Temple:

> Now in the first year of Cyrus king of Persia, that the word of the Lord spoken by the mouth of Jeremiah might be accomplished, the Lord stirred up the spirit of Cyrus king of Persia,

that he made a proclamation throughout all his kingdom, and put it also in writing, saying, "Thus saith Cyrus king of Persia, All the kingdoms of the earth hath the Lord God of heaven given me; and he hath charged me to build an house in Jerusalem, which is in Judah Who is there among you of all his people? The Lord his God be with him, and let him go up."

Though himself a Gentile, Cyrus' great human rights decree had permitted exiled Jews to leave their captivity in Babylon, along with all their possessions, and return to Jerusalem.[7]

After arriving in Tehran, Jane made a conscientious effort to study Persian history even in the midst of her busy teaching schedule. Her arrival in 1921 enabled her to witness some of the greatest changes that ever came to Iran.

In 1921, Reza Khan Pahlavi, a cavalryman, marched his 3,000 men ninety miles from Qazvin into Tehran, the capital city, and took control of the government. He became Prime Minister in 1923 and by 1925 founded the new Pahlavi dynasty as shah.[8] Reza Shah was a tall, rugged, formidable man who was ambitious for his country. Soon after taking control, he began to introduce sweeping programs of change, hoping to bring Persia into the twentieth century and make it more difficult for other countries to interfere in Persia's internal affairs. During his reign, he rebuilt the armed forces, encouraged industry, organized a national bank, developed a transportation system, built a cross-country railroad, and enacted new civil and criminal codes patterned after French law. He induced women to cast aside their veils, built new schools and hospitals and founded the University of Tehran. In addition, he reduced the authority of the clergy and sought restrictions on tribal activities. Under his rule, Persia began to establish its identity under its own name of Iran, rather than the one Greek writers had used centuries before.[9]

In the midst of the turmoil of World War II, Reza Shah was forced to abdicate in favor of his twenty-two year old son, Mohammad Reza Pahlavi,[10] who endeavored to continue many of his father's reforms. He modified some (allowing women to choose whether or not to wear the chador); accelerated others (urging increased education and expanded roles and rights for women); and inaugurated great social and economic changes through his "White Revolution" program. The White Revolution touched the lives of almost every citizen in some way.

In the course of these changes, powerful and violent opposition arose. There are hundreds of explanations as to why Mohammad Reza Pahlavi eventually fell from power and was forced to leave his homeland with his family. The underlying issues were longstanding and equally numerous, and, as events revealed, overpowering. The deeply religious Iranians, accustomed to honoring a father figure, welcomed a new ruler in the person of the Ayatollah Rubollah Khomeini, a Muslim mullah leader of the Islamic Revolution.[11]

Jane is probably the only American woman who lived in Tehran before the inception of the Pahlavi dream of building a strong independent, sectarian Iran and stayed to see its cataclysmic collapse. Each change would affect Jane Doolittle's life incredibly. But the young American girl who gave herself to God's loving service in Iran made her lifetime journey in a day-by-day walk. She steadfastly placed her trust in God.

But then, in November of 1921, Jane's biggest concern was not having heard from her family for three weeks. None of the teachers had received any mail. According to one knowledgeable woman from the British legation, "This is nothing. Wait until winter; that's when mail just simply does not get through." Nonetheless, Jane continued writing her weekly letters home. She began to wonder what Thanksgiving and Christmas would be like in Persia. If Jane were home she would likely spend Thanksgiving in Wallingford, Connecticut, at her Aunt Jennie's. She and her sister, Catherine, and her brothers, Jed and Nat, would carry out a favorite tradition of searching around in the roomy old attic for the mince pies hidden there for discovery. Would she get mince pie this year? She wasn't even sure that Iran Bethel scheduled time for this purely American custom of Thanksgiving.

However, the Saturday before Thanksgiving, Charlotte rushed in to tell her that they had been invited to spend the night with the Wyshams to help prepare for a big Thanksgiving celebration. School would close to suggest to the students the importance of setting aside a particular day to thank God for all His blessings. Pleased and excited, the young women hurried over to the Wyshams who also lived at the central compound. Will and Miriam

Wysham[12] had arrived in Tehran just a few months before Charlotte. Jane had met them at the weekly station prayer meeting, but other than that they hadn't had much opportunity to socialize.

"Oh, you'll enjoy them, Jane" promised Charlotte. "Miriam's a southerner who couldn't imagine what she'd ever do in place like this. But believe me, she's done so many lovely things for us. And Will! He's fun and brilliant—he's absorbing the Persian language like a sponge."

What a hilarious time they had preparing for Thanksgiving, such as when Charlotte made soapy fudge. The Wysham's freight had only just arrived and, unfortunately, the cocoa and soap had been put into the same packing box, resulting now in Charlotte's soapy-tasting fudge. With a gleeful twinkle in his eyes, Will held aloft his brown, barely bitten, piece of bitter fudge and announced, "It's really more than I can swallow!" He tossed it smack into the wastebasket. To prove it hadn't been the cook's fault, Charlotte started over with untainted ingredients and made a second batch that was a rich and delicious success.

Thanksgiving night Jane helped Charlotte tie the sash on her rose crepe dress and pronounced her elegant. Jane and Miriam were equally stunning in their black gowns, and Lillian wore a very becoming pink. The Ingleside residents furnished the potatoes, creamed onions and soup for the meal. There were also three wild turkeys[13] glazed into golden brown perfection, and other traditional Thanksgiving fare, including mince pie as moist and spicy as Jane's Aunt Jennie's. Together, the nineteen guests meditated upon David's thanksgiving Psalm:

> Give thanks unto the Lord, call upon his name, make known
> his deeds among the people. Sing unto him, sing psalms unto
> him, talk ye of all his wondrous works . . . . For great is the
> Lord, and greatly to be praised . . . (I Chron. 16:8, 9, 25).

Jane and Charlotte were especially grateful that year for their new friendship. In fact, Charlotte had just written her family that:

> . . . The finest thing that happened this week for me has been
> finding a friend, one of the real kind, in Jane. Oh, how fortu-
> nate I am and how wonderful is the God who knows and pre-
> pares just the right thing at the right time. I surely am to be en-

vied in having such strong and inspiring companions as Jane
and Lillian . . . .

It rained continually for the next several days after Thanksgiving. The gloomy weather, together with concern for the lack of
news from home, and the realization that many of them would
be spending their first Christmas away from their families,
caused the young women to be homesick. But soon the sun
pushed through the overcast sky, brightening their world con-
siderably. However, the teachers knew that if they were going to
get into the Christmas spirit in this land, they would have to gen-
erate it themselves.

"Joy to the world, the Lord has come!" Charlotte sang as Jane
came into the room.

"That sounds fine," said Jane.

"What about 'We Three Kings of Orient Are'?" asked Lillian
joining them.

"Along that line," added Jane, "what about 'The First Noel'
which tells of the star that drew the three wise men 'to the northwest?'

O'er Bethlehem it took its rest,
to seek a king was their intent,
And to follow the star wherever it went.'

"I have a whole new feeling for stars since that long night out
there on the desert a couple months ago."

Miss Peet, whom everyone called Peter, entered the room and
responded to Jane's comment. "Do you know, Jane, that we are
less than a hundred miles from the town where it is believed that
the Wise Men commenced their long journey to Jerusalem?"

"Really?" exclaimed Jane.

"Yes, and it's kind of awesome, isn't it," said Peter, settling
into an easy chair. "The Wise Men and their history are somewhat complicated, and I'm not an authority on their practices;
however, our Scriptures give a brief comment in Matthew 2, and
here, in Persia, there are many legends and traditions. So, according to legend, the town of Saveh is where the travel to Jerusalem
and Bethlehem began. The Wise Men studied and searched the
stars, believing that they could fathom the future from them.
And when they saw the Star of Bethlehem, about which they had

studied, they knew that a king was born. Then they collected together gold, frankincense and myrrh,[14] to carry to Him to show their honor and respect."

"Isn't it amazing," said Charlotte, "to think that the Persian Magi[15] could have come through here on their way to honor the Son of God. Imagine plodding all those miles to Bethlehem on their camels, following the light of the Star. They knew why they were going to that far-off land, just as we know why we've come here to this far-off land—to honor that very same King.

"But those Wise Men came away not ever recognizing Him as the Most High God. They never really came to know Him at all.

"'Yet a little while is the light with you. Walk while ye have the light lest darkness come upon you, for he that walketh in darkness knoweth not whither he goeth. While ye have light, believe in the light, that ye may be children of the light'" (Jn. 12: 35, 36).

"And how remarkable," said Jane, "that Christ's birth came about exactly as foretold by the prophet Isaiah some 700 years previously" (Is. 7:14).

"What about the Magi and their connection with Zoroastrianism?" asked Jane. "Wasn't that Persia's national religion before Muhammad, an Arab, brought his foreign faith here in the seventh century?"

"Well, yes," responded Miss Peet. "But like many other peoples, it is believed that the Persians first worshipped the elements of nature—the sun, sky, water, fire, air and earth—and the related gods and goddesses who were believed to have control of those forces. How did one please these powers? What sacrifices and appeasements were to be made? To find an answer the Persians dealt with the occult, with superstition and with both magical and mystical rites. They also wore amulets and ornamental charms—often with special inscriptions—to ward off evil and disease or to bring good fortune to the wearer. Persia has long been the land of speculative thinkers. The prophet Muhammad said that 'If learning were suspended at the highest parts of Heaven, the Persians would attain it.'

"Then, some say that about 2500 years ago, Zardusht or Zarathrustra, called Zoroaster by the Greeks, came and preached of one god. Zardusht is thought to have been born in northeast Per-

sia about 600 B.C.[16] He is said to have been an unusual child
who began having visions very early. At about age thirty he began to preach his new religion of one god, 'Ahura Mazda,' and of
one opposing evil force, 'Ahriman.' The Magi are believed to
have belonged to an ancient cult of Zarathustrian priests. They
regarded fire as a reflection of their deity; it symbolized moral
purity and was a strong weapon of defense against the demons
round about them.

"It is said that a Persian king named 'Vishtaspa' accepted
these beliefs after his queen had done so, and adopted them for
his court. The early monarchs of the Persian Empire, such as
King Darius and his successors, supported Zarathustrian beliefs.
After Alexander the Macedonian conquered Persia (330 B.C.),
this monotheistic religion died out for awhile. But it once again
became the national religion during Sassanian times (226-641
A.D.) and lasted until the Muslim Arabs defeated the Sassanians
and introduced Islam (641 A.D.)."

"Well," said Jane, "all I can say is that the more I hear about
Persia, the more I want to learn."

At this season of year, Jane was thankful for her winter woo-
lies, high-topped shoes and warm hats. Not that it was colder in
Tehran than in New York, but the lack of central heating made it
seem so. It snowed shortly before Christmas, and this soft while
mantle brightened the place, lending brief beauty to the mud-
brown scenery.

Preparing for Christmas in a non-Christian land was a new experience for Jane. There were no cheery Christmas lights, no gar-
lands of green or wreaths with red ribbons and shiny gold balls;
no carolers, no bells; and no children standing in line to see Santa
Claus.

"How different this is," said Jane to Charlotte as they tried to
locate a shop where they might find a few last-minute gifts to
place under their Christmas tree. Sometimes they'd pass an object that looked like a bagged-up bundle of old rags pressed
against a wall. But upon looking more closely, they'd see a head
and realize it was a woman. Jane also noticed groups of dirty
and ragged children crowded in half-boarded doorways. They
seemed to her to be nothing more than enormous, staring eyes.
"Do they ever have proper food and care?" she asked.

"Probably not," sighed Charlotte. "There are so many families who have only $100 to live on for a whole year. As with most underdeveloped nations, there are so many simultaneous needs that it weighs everyone down. There are rich people here, and there are also the desperately poor. These two extremes do not often come in touch with each other. There are practically no agencies or other organized programs of help; individuals aid the individual poor whom they personally know. A number of Christians here have been very concerned about the poor and are trying to help."

"Oh my," sighed Jane, "there's so much to be done, isn't there?"

"Yes," continued Charlotte, "there's great distress here. Not that we don't have it in our own country—I've seen it and been involved with it. Poverty is heartbreaking wherever it is."

Wordlessly, they turned back toward the mission compound. They hadn't found all their gifts, but they were thinking of the One Gift-giver.

For Jane, it was exactly a year since she had said "Yes, Lord, I'll go to Iran Bethel if that's Your plan." It was also almost a year since Charlotte had left her family. The two liked sharing these experiences with each other, for each needed the other to be the family that was now so far away.

"How thankful I am for such a wonderful friend," Jane thought. Remembering the wretched poor she had just seen, she added "and for having a comfortable place to live."

For their own special touch of Christmas delight, Jane and the other Inglesiders rose at 5:00 A.M. Christmas day to go caroling. Bundling up from head to toe, they piled into the doroshgeh they'd hired. Joyously they clopped over the snow to the nearby residence of the American Charge' d' Affaires. There, in the chilly stillness of the early dawn, they dared to break the silence with their jubilant proclamations: "Hark! the herald angels sing, Glory to the newborn king . . . ."

Very soon they were rewarded by seeing an upstairs window push open. The night-shirted Charge' d'Affaires called out cheerfully, "Angels! Angels! Thank you for your early morning visitation. Merry, merry Christmas to you. We look forward to seeing you later. Sing on, sing on!"

After a couple more songs, they went back to the compound. As they sang "Dashing through the snow, in a one-horse open sleigh . . . ," their song was accompanied by the rhythmic clippity-clop of their two-horse doroshgeh.

At noon, all the missionaries, dressed in their festive best, gathered at the home of Dr. and Mrs. Samuel Jordan[17] to share a candlelit Christmas dinner with all the trimmings. The celebration included an exchange of gifts, and then, the most wonderful surprise of all. The doorbell rang and there stood the mission servant with a huge gunny-sack full of mail! The contents spilled out of the bulging bag all over the floor, and in scarcely more than a split second, everyone was down on hands and knees scrambling for Christmas letters and cards from home. For Jane, there came an unexpected surprise: her Wells friends and faculty had designed and sent a beautiful memory book. For each day of the year there was a page offering a favorite poem or Scripture and a personal word of remembrance and encouragement. In the ensuing years, this loving token of friendship became one of Jane's prized treasures.

On New Year's the Inglesiders had callers from morning until night, serving them tea, nuts, candies, cakes and fruit. Nineteen twenty-two was starting with new friends, new vigor and renewed joy.

NOTES

1. The American Mission Hospital was the birthplace of Farah Diba. At age twenty-one she became Empress Farah, the "shahbanou" (queen) of Iran. During World War II, the hospital was closed by the mission board. Thereafter, the U.S. government used it as a hospital and recreational center. Finally it became the campus for the Community School which served English-speaking children.

2. Mary Slessor, known as the "White Ma" of Calabar, was a Scots Presbyterian missionary. This Scottish factory girl served in Calabar for thirty-eight years (1848-1915). She developed people's industrial capacities, built churches and schools, helped to bring law and order, raised the status of African women and educated many to a Christian way of life. She was influenced greatly by David Livingstone (1813-1873). He, too, had been a textile worker in a Scottish town not far from hers before he embarked on his missionary adventures.

3. Generally, the Persians followed a traditional custom of standing over a hole in the floor or ground and squatting. For cleansing they used an "aftabeh", a pitcher-like vessel with a curved spout which held water for washing one's self. Jane, however, had been advised to bring a three-year supply of toilet tissue and it had been a mini-adventure to calculate, purchase, pack and transport such a quantity.

4. Men carried on similar bathing practices in their bathing quarters, but were required to cover their genitalia at all times. They'd soak, scrub, relax and visit, finding great enjoyment in each other's company. However, instead of bathing all day, the men's baths took only a few hours. Some wealthier families had private baths in their homes. These were tiled, elevated slabs on which one could lie while being scrubbed by an attendant.

5. The gates of the city were locked at 5:00 P.M.

6. Persians bought a twelve to fourteen-inch tall sugar cone which they chopped with a hatchet-like instrument into many small pieces. These were never as large as American small sugar cubes.

7. The human rights declaration of Cyrus the Great has been miraculously preserved on its baked-earth cylinder. It was found in 1879 by archaeologists working in Mesopotamia. This is housed in the British Museum in London while a copy of the original may be found in a museum in Tehran. A part of the declaration, translated from the Babylonian text (inscribed in cuneiform characters), reads:

> I, Cyrus, King of Kings, son of Cambyses, grandson of Cyrus, whose dynasty has been blessed by the gods and whose reign is based upon the heart, when I entered the city of Babylon all the people welcomed me with joy. I assumed the throne of the king. Marduk, the god of Babel, whom I have taken in and whom I have loved, won the noble hearts of the people of Babel for me. My great army entered this city without incident. The holy places of the city moved my heart. I accorded to all men the freedom to worship their own gods and ordered that no one had the right to bother them. I ordered that no house be destroyed, that no inhabitant be dispossessed. The great god accorded to me and to all my army his benefits. From Babel to Assur, from Susa to Addak . . . , and in all the regions inhabited on the other side of the Tigris, I wished that all the temples that had been closed be reopened, that all the statues of the gods be returned to their place, and that they remain there forever. I reassembled the inhabitants of these regions and had their houses, which had been destroyed, rebuilt. I saw that the gods of Sumer and Akkad were returned to their places which are called "the joy of the hearts." I accorded peace and quiet to all men.

8. In 1915 Reza Khan married Taj-ol-Muluk, the daughter of an army officer. A daughter, Shams, was born. On October 26, 1919, twins arrived. The boy, Mohammad Reza, was destined to be heir to the throne; the girl, Princess Ashraf.

9. "Fars," a name which originally applied only to the province of Fars in the south.

10. Iran proclaimed its neutrality in both World War I and II. However, during the Second War the Allies needed Iran's oil and use of the Trans-Iranian Railway to ship supplies to Russia. The Allies demanded that Reza Shah expel some 690 German nationals who were working in Iran as technicians for the Iranian government, insisting that these Germans might compromise Iran's neutrality and act against the Allied interests. Reza Shah refused, and on August 25, 1941, the British occupied southern Iran and the Russians occupied the north.

11. Fifteen years previously, Khomeini had been exiled because of his agitation against the shah's policies of land reform, modernization,and the emancipation of women. On February 1, 1979, Khomeini's return was greeted by thousands of jubilant demonstrators. More than ninety percent of Iran's fifty million people belong to the Shi'aism branch of Islam.

12. Dr. William N. Wysham received his B.A. from Lafayette College (Phi Beta Kappa, class valedictorian) and his M.A. from Princeton. A graduate of Princeton Theological Seminary, he received an honorary D.D. from Coe College. Dr. Wysham served the United Presbyterian Church for forty-two years as a missionary and an executive. While in Iran (1920-1938), he served on the faculty of Alborz College and was responsible for the production, publication and distribution of Christian materials for use in many Middle Eastern countries. He traveled extensively throughout Asia and Africa and served on many interdenominational committees.

13. Turkeys were not native to Persia.

14. According to Christian tradition, gold is a symbol of Christ's Diety, frankincense a symbol of the purity of Christ's life, and myrrh a burial spice symbolizing His suffering.

15. The Magi were astrologers who studied and specialized in astrology, medicine and natural science. "Magian" is an Iranian word meaning the use of means, such as charms or spells, believed to have supernatural power over natural forces. An early pagan cult, it was perhaps later taken over by Zoroastrianism.

16. According to the Zoroastrian Center in Anaheim, California, Zoroaster is said to have been born around 1767 B.C. Zoroaster is the most current of various Greek forms for his first name, Zarathustra. He was one of the earliest sages to teach monotheism, the belief in one God. He preached a new doctrine of good, evil and retribution and used as his triple motto "Good Thoughts, Good Words, Good Deeds." The Zoroastrian religion had spread all over the Iranian plateau by the sixth century B.C. It was instrumental in the founding of the first world empire by the Achaemenians under Cyrus the Great, around 550 B.C. This empire was not bound by linguistic or ethnic frontiers. Whereas earlier conquests had meant the total destruction of the vanquished, the Achaemenians were politically, religiously and ethnically tolerant. When Cyrus, thought to be a follower of Zoroaster, conquered Babylon in 539 B.C., he freed all captive peoples, including the Jews who had remained in bondage there for seventy years.

17. Dr. Samuel Jordan, distinguished American educator, was president of the Alborz High School and College (for men) between 1925 and 1949. Jordan Boulevard, an important thoroughfare in Tehran, was named in his honor, but since Khomeini's return it has been renamed.

CHAPTER THREE

Expanding Circles of Love

With the beginning of hot weather in the middle of May, classes started before 7:00 A.M. and ended at noon. Jane had been wondering about the possibility of having a summer camp for the girls. She discussed the idea with the other teachers and all thought it was a plan worth trying. Jane began making arrangements. Weeks later, Tehran news would carry a story stating that:

> In 1922, Miss Jane Doolittle organized a first girls' summer camp. She and 26 girls walked from the school to Dezashub, Shrimran. It took them from 5:00 until 9:30 A.M. They stayed one month and did all their own cooking and chores as well as having athletic activities and daily lessons. Then they walked back to Tehran, but, of course, the trip was easier. It was downhill!

The camp was, indeed, newsworthy. In the first place, it was extraordinary for fathers to trust their daughters with non-relatives for that length of time. Next, the girls had never had any experience of this kind—nor had their teachers. Charlotte shared her enthusiasm about the camp with her family in a letter:

> . . . School is closing the first of next week and we will be off for the mountains, ten miles up the country, where it will be more comfortable and where the nights will always be cool. We have secured two gardens, almost adjoining. This is an entirely new thing for Persian girls and we are delighted that as many as twenty girls are going to take advantage of the splendid opportunity. Our three-year teacher from Wells is manager, financier and everything. Wells College girls have surely been good to us and if it were not for them we would not be having our camp nor a new and very badly needed playground for next

year. How we wish the camp could be a permanent thing. The girls can scarcely wait to get started and it is such a pity that some of the Persian girls we would most like to go are not allowed only because it is not the custom and people might talk . . .

The walk that took them from the central compound to their camping site was a distance of perhaps ten miles. But just picking up and putting down one foot after another in a steady constant uphill walk was a totally new experience for the Persian girls. They weren't used to much walking, and the teachers had to do a lot of singing to help keep them moving.

For twenty-three year old Jane it had been only a couple of years since she and five of her Wells' classmates had decided to walk the seventeen miles between Aurora and Auburn, New York, to meet some other friends for lunch. Esther Cox recalls the event:

> It was a long grueling morning and when we reached town and found curbs on the streets, we could hardly change our pace to accommodate them. Jane was very tired and had some pain in her hips, but never complained a bit. We spent the night in the home of our Bible professor and were happy to join the other girls in taking the train back to college.

Camping in Persia didn't mean going into the woods with a camper or pitching a tent on a grassy spot for a few days. It meant renting quarters up-country. This turned out to be a nice garden place with an old, two-story mansion and an outside kitchen. Renting the house and garden cost a total of 125 "tomans"—about $125 for three months; a lot of money in those days. Since Wells College was sponsoring Jane, they provided the money for the rent. Indeed, Wells was supportive of all that Jane was doing, and, in the future, would help in many ways to develop Jane's expanding work at Iran Bethel.

At this first outdoor educational summer camp, called "Progress Camp," the students and teachers did the cooking. Jane remembers that some of the meals "weren't very good." They also took turns doing the chores. One of Charlotte's letters home (July 12, 1922), gives some interesting details about the students' response to camp:

> . . . It has so far been full of all the interesting things that it

promised to be except that Jane had to go and get a three-day
fever and that sort of disrupted things for the girls. They look
to her for everything and when she wasn't here they got a rather lost feeling—something like it is when mother gets sick at
home. I tried to look after things and see that everybody was
fed and put to bed in the proper way and that they had some
daily exercise in the form of a walk or some games, but, I too
felt sort of lost and wanted to do all I could to make Jane more
comfy, if such a thing were possible with these horrid fevers
that have to run their course. Naturally, things didn't go the
same. However, things by that time were in very good running
order—the cooks, dishwashers and table-girls knowing just
what they were supposed to be doing—so it wasn't too bad.
And now Jane is all well again—or at least she says she is— and
we are not worrying anymore . . . .

I told you that the girls are supposed to speak nothing but English here. They have a good deal of fun over it but already I am
noticing an improvement and if for that reason only the whole
proposition would be worthwhile. But I am sure there will be
more worthwhile results . . . .

The plan is to have an all-day picnic every week. By "all-day"
picnic, we mean getting up at 3:30 or 4:00 A.M. and returning
at 7:00 P.M. And by "picnic" we also mean a hike and not food
as the word usually means at home. Food is merely a necessary
evil. "Sangak" (Persian bread), cucumbers, eggs, cheese and to-
matoes were the bill of fare for the one I want to tell you about
that we took last week.

We started off with 17 girls, 2 servants and 3 donkeys. There is
always the samovar that has to be taken and they always are so
bunglesome—food for a crowd like that takes up space—and
there never being any grass to sit on, we always have to take a
rug or two with us so you can see how we would need at least
one donkey . . . . We walked upward for two hours following
the course of one of the rare mountain streams bordered with
"green things" growing so naturally and woodsy as to make
one feel they had accidentally stepped from Persia back to the
woods and hills of childhood days in Ohio.

It made me feel like staying until suddenly we turned a curve
in the road and came upon one of those little mountain villages
built in such a way as to make the houses look like so many
sandhills projecting from the slope. The people, although pictu-

resque, look so unkempt and dirty—just like the straggly, grimy chickens that live all over their streets and in their houses. In that one little walk we saw so many pitiable human wrecks—absolutely hopeless as to any future bodily comfort on account of deformation, a blind or sore eye, etc. I thought of the Master and what He would have done for them had He been passing by, and wondered how much it would change their hopeless attitude should they really find Him now?

After the first two hours' climb, we got permission to enter a lovely garden bordering the stream—it would be hard to describe the place, suffice it to say that it was a green slope covered for the most part with cherry trees and we basked several hours in the shade listening to the gushing music of the mountain stream at the foot of the slope. Our donkey had to be left there while we, loading the pack of food and necessaries on our own shoulders, began a very steep, rocky climb toward the waterfalls which was our final destination. Just before reaching the coveted spot we had the thrilling experience of helping a bunch of terrified, inexperienced girls down a rather steep and precipitous path that acted as though it was going to roll all its stones down the valley every time you stepped on one . . . . It was scary, but all made it safely!

After lunch, supervised by their faithful Sahok, and a siesta, the group began the return trip from the picnic. With Charlotte leading, and all shoes in hand, they began by wading through a steam. When Sahok slipped on a wet rock, the girls were in shock for their own safety; but between Jane's calming effectiveness and Charlotte's training as a Girl Scout guide, the "wilderness" adventure became an exciting tale of a day with nature "in the rough."

Another camping event, "Stunt Night", turned out to be a success of even greater significance for the creative talents and teamwork of the students were impressive. American missionary ladies, living nearby, were guests for the performance of clever skits, songs, dialogues and papers.

In describing that night Charlotte wrote about the students:

[Degranuhi is] . . . one of the liveliest wires we have, as well as one of the most lovable, jolly, bubbling girls you ever knew. It is a joy to think of her and the way her high-pitched, incongruous voice . . . keep the rest of the girls livened up. She broadcasts her love and beaming face but her special love is Jane, and when the latter was sick, because Degranuhi was down in spirits the effect on others was at once apparent. However, this girl couldn't be entirely squelched and when I took pity on her and let her help me do something for her adored Miss Doolittle, we heard her go back into the room with the others and in an exaggeratedly awed tone, not meant for our ears, and that sent the girls into gales of laughter, say, "I saw her—girls—she looked just like an angel!" And then, to her rival for first place in Jane's affections, "Christine—I'm very sorry for you!" Christine, too, is a lovable girl but of a very different type, so sensitive, impressionable, moody, yet very thoughtful, kind and loyal . . . .

And Arpinik, so dependable, steady, sensible and so very kindhearted. She showed us best what she really is by the way she did her part on stunt night. Practically everything that happened behind the scenes she was being called for, but she never appeared on the stage except to sing in a final song. It turned out that she had composed the song, had made most of the funny costumes and helped the little girls get their parts ready. That's Arpinik.

Charlotte also wrote about the activities at the end of the day:

You might enjoy coming up the moonlight path some of these fine nights about 9:00 and sitting at the foot of the steps to listen to the interested group of 24 girls seated about the long table. They are thinking, for as their leader (Miss Doolittle) changes those familiar "why, what fors and whens" of the chemistry classroom into questions that vitally concern their spiritual lives and their relations to their great friend Christ, [Jane] is getting answers. Bedtime comes and there are always things left over to the next night. That is something to look forward to! These informal discussions of the evening hour and the lovely hymns . . . we hope will be among the most pleasant of camp memories.

Goli, now a grown woman with grandchildren, remembers vividly just how she felt about summer camp when it was her turn to go:

It was the most exciting thing that ever happened. I was so afraid that my father wouldn't let me go. I was almost sleepless for days until he finally decided that he could trust Miss Doolittle and the teachers and the whole adventure . . . . Of course, there were very strict rules. We could not leave the premises of our garden (a big place) without approval from Miss Doolittle and we had to be in the care of one of the other teachers. I almost died when it was reported that I had left camp without approval. Miss Doolittle called me in. She said she was going to call my father and have someone come and take me home right then and there. I'd only been there five days. Such agony—but when the matter was explained to Miss Doolittle that I had misunderstood, not being present when that regulation was discussed, and had unknowingly disobeyed the rule, she said it would be all right just so I never did it again—which, of course, I didn't.

We had an absolutely marvelous time—one that brings me some of the happiest memories of my girlhood. I will never cease to thank Miss Doolittle for her teaching and love. My father was a professor and so he had much respect for the education that Miss Doolittle and the others in Iran Bethel, or the American School as we often called it, were giving us. She is beloved!

At the conclusion of their first summer camp, the teachers walked the girls back downhill to Tehran, and saw each one happily and safely returned to her parents. Then Jane, Charlotte and Lillian went back to the summer camp for a short time to enjoy the peace and quiet. Miss Peet had left on furlough and Lillian McHenry become the new principal. Jane, though, was still under-the-weather from her earlier fever. On August 17, 1922, the camp welcomed the birth of James Kemp Wysham, the first of the Wysham's four children. For Jane, that date had particular meaning: exactly one year before, she had left her home and family in New York to come to Persia.

The summer days were now exceedingly hot and humid. With the heat came depression, and home seemed like such a wonderful place to be. During the ensuing weeks, Charlotte sensed that Jane was still homesick and tried to think of ways to cheer her along. Finally, one day, she decided to confide her concerns with Jane's mother. Weeks later, Charlotte received a reply from Mr. Doolittle.

October 21, 1922
40 Rider Street
New York City

My Dear Charlotte:

I have been deeply touched by the letter you wrote "Jane's mother" which she handed me to read. Jane's letters have been so full of enthusiasm and an encouraging happy side of her work that we have had no information that there was another side she is keeping hidden from us. We were hoping that her work so filled her thoughts that there would not be time for homesickness, but it is almost inevitable that many discouraging things will come up when face to face with such a big problem as you have on your hands. I hope Jane will speedily banish from her mind that there is any thing in the wide world she cannot tell her mother. I fear she feels we are not entirely in sympathy with her work. But this is a natural mistake which comes from our attitude when she first began to talk Persia.

We wanted her to use her life to the very best advantage in the Master's service, but we felt that a girl of 22 was too young to go away so far beyond any possible help from her family. We wanted her to wait a few years until she was older and more mature, spending the time as she wanted to in study or other kinds of useful service. But it was the enthusiasm of youth against the conservation of years, and youth won. When her decision was made we simply did the best we could to equip her and send her on her happy way. I'm afraid Jane interpreted our anxiety for her into opposition to her work. In this she is mistaken for we are very proud of her and what she is doing. The world is full of suffering and misery and the work you girls are doing in brightening and uplifting the lives of those Persian girls fills us with admiration. We who are here at home only desire to do what we can to make your self-doing efforts more efficient and your lives happier.

I have written you very frankly in order that you may have the key to Jane's feelings—our differences of opinion all belong to the past and should be forgotten. We want to help her in every way possible and do rejoice with her in the success of her efforts.

We are very grateful that she has such a close, congenial friend as you are, Charlotte. I know it helps her and it helps us too. We are not very formidable people, so write us whenever you feel inclined.

Yours affectionately,
"Jane's Dad"

On October 28, 1923, exactly two years after Jane arrived in Persia, Reza Khan became the Prime Minister. There was keen interest and speculation among the people as they discussed hopes that their world could settle into a more stable pattern.

During this time Jane wasn't well, still bothered by lingering effects of the infection she'd contracted during the first summer camp. In January, the school decided to send her away for a month's rest at Rasht, northeast of Tehran. Since young women did not travel alone in those days, Elgin Sherk, another missionary, accompanied her on the ten to twelve-hour journey to the Caspian Sea. There, she stayed with the Paul Shedds who had crossed the Atlantic with her on the "S.S. City of York." They lived next door to Dr. John Frame who directed the big mission hospital in that area. He supervised treatments for Jane. At the end of the month, she returned to Tehran and carried on with her work, as usual. However, she hadn't gained as much strength as she had hoped during her vacation.

In May of 1924, near the end of her three-year term, the staff advised Jane to return home for health reasons. She left, sad at heart at having to miss the June commencement. The students were even sadder than she. "Come back, come back! Hurry back, Miss Doolittle!" they urged. And, indeed, with Miss McHenry's leaving as principal, the mission asked Jane if she would consider returning as principal of Iran Bethel.

Would she be back? "There's a young woman whose health will never permit her to return to Persia," concluded Jean Wells, an R.N. just returning from furlough to her post in northern Persia. The two had met as strangers on the road to Kermanshah. In those days of little traffic, most cars stopped to greet the other, hoping to see a friend. Jean and Jane had asked their drivers to stop as they traveled across Persia's flat dry landscape. A new friendship was born.

However, Jane's homeward journey was not along the usual Russian or Indian route, but on a new caravan route that had just been opened from Baghdad to Damascus. She was the first of the missionaries to make this rugged desert trek, and the only woman in the five-car caravan. The first two long, hot days and nights were across an arid, desolate,wind-blown expanse of shifting sand. There were no roads, no hotels, no cafes, no restrooms and no other people. The drivers calculated their direction by compass, keeping in sight of one another so that none would stray off and become lost.

But for Jane, going toward Damascus was exciting, even if slow and wearying. With the appearance of green trees and shrubs came a thrilling thought: Saul, the brilliant young Jewish man, probably about her own age, had journeyed to Damascus from Jerusalem some nineteen hundred years earlier.

A zealous follower of God, Saul was nonetheless filled with

hatred and evil intent toward Christ and the early Christians. A keenly analytical thinker (a student of Gamaliel, a highly respected leader of Israel), Saul left Jerusalem "breathing out threatenings and slaughter against the disciples of the Lord. He went up to the high priest and desired of him letters to Damascus, the synagogues, that if he found any of the way [believers in Christ], whether they were men or women, he might bring them bound to Jerusalem" (Acts 9:1, 2).

But as Saul drew near Damascus, he had a sudden and dramatic encounter—" . . . there shined round about him a light from heaven . . . " (Acts 9:3). The result left him stunned and blind. Led by the hand into Damascus, Saul had fasted and waited for three days until God's messenger came to him. When his sight was restored and he was filled with the Holy Spirit, Saul began his long ministry of preaching that Jesus was the Son of God! After this miraculous conversion, Saul was renamed Paul, and became known as the great missionary to the Gentiles.

Many early Christians followed Christ's command to preach the gospel (good news). Jane knew from the Bible record that Persians were in Jerusalem for the Feast of Pentecost (a Greek word) when the Holy Spirit manifested Himself to Jesus' followers. Some of those Persians had believed the life-changing story of Christ's love for all people and carried the good news back to their homeland. Jane liked to think of herself, a young American missionary, as another one in the long Christian continuum responding to Christ's Great Commission, "Go ye into all the world and preach the gospel . . . " (Mark 16:15a).

Leaving Damascus, Jane traveled throughout the Holy Land, a place of deep significance to Christians, Muslims and Jews alike. She found it to be a profound and enriching experience to walk in the land where Jesus was born, raised and had begun His earthly ministry. The experience strengthened Jane's commitment to serve her Lord.

Traveling on, she took a train to Alexandria, Egypt, from where she sailed to Marseille. Again traveling by train, she met her sister, Catherine, in Paris. Catherine was living in the city as an art student. Together, they toured England and Scotland before Jane boarded the ocean liner, "Majestic," for home.

Steaming into New York harbor in early June, 1924, was even

more exciting than Jane had anticipated. There, standing tall and stately, was the welcoming Statue of Liberty. "How thrilling to be home again in the land of my forefathers" she thought!

During her three-year absence, Jane had missed her family most. But now, seeing the busy port, the skyscrapers, and all the sights, and hearing the sounds of New York, Jane was struck by a new thought: "A woman in America can make more choices for herself than a woman anywhere else in the world." She thought of the big choice that faced her now: would she give up her long-held dream of becoming a doctor in Africa and go back to Persia, spending her life, instead, as an educator? She looked forward to talking and praying with her parents about her next step.

Her father, mother and brother, Nat, were at the wharf to meet her. How good it was to embrace her family and bask in their warm welcome. Her bright, cheerful mother and gentle, thoughtful father hadn't changed. How pleasant to be home and enjoy her father's flourishing flower and vegetable gardens and all their many questions about Persia and its culture. Only one thing seemed to mar the present and threaten the future—the question of Jane's health.

She soon began making the rounds to various specialists in New York. She had digestive problems which had bothered her frequently in Persia, and severe back pains continued to be a source of great discomfort. At the New York Orthopedic Hospital Jane underwent innumerable tests, x-rays and examinations. The specialists finally concluded that the fourth lumbar vertebra was out of place. Dr. Hibbs, head of the hospital, had found that this condition, later known as "a slipped disc", could be improved by fusing the problem vertebrae. Jane requested that Dr. Hibbs perform the operation and he did. In subsequent years, Dr. Hibbs insisted that Jane was his patient, and thereafter, performed all her needed orthopedic surgery.

Jane accepted the doctors' diagnosis as a factor to be considered in discerning God's plan for her in His work. In Persia she'd observed Dr. Frame's life at close range. She was keenly aware of the constant physical demands shouldered by a missionary doctor. Tremendous energy and stamina were needed, as well as wisdom, skill and patience, to meet the responsibilities of this profession. Perhaps Jane's physical limitations were God's way of redirecting her goals?

Since she'd been invited to assume the principalship of Iran Bethel, and since she loved the girls and her work among them, perhaps God was leading her to continue in His service in Persia instead of Africa, and by way of education rather than medicine? Her father and mother concurred with her reasoning.

Thus, Jane Doolittle, at this crossroad, abandoned pursuit of her medical career and set about to prepare for a new profession in education. Jane would return to Tehran!

CHAPTER FOUR

New Horizons

Jane enrolled at Columbia University, living at Seth Hall, the dormitory for graduate students. She began work toward a Master's degree in Educational Administration to better equip her for the principalship at Iran Bethel. And, to further enhance her abilities, she commenced studies at the Biblical Seminary in New York (later known as the New York Theological Seminary).

Jane's three-year absence from New York heightened her awareness of an accelerating tempo in the land. The rousing war songs she remembered from her college days had given way to the "Roaring '20s" and the Charleston dance. Henry Ford was shocking the world with an eight-hour, five-day work-week schedule. Airmail service between New York and Boston began. Calvin Coolidge was president and women were experiencing for the first time the thrill of voting in a national election.

Women's abilities were beginning to be recognized and used in broader and more varied fields. While a student at Wells, Jane had learned of activities in behalf of equal rights for women. Just across the lake from Aurora, in Seneca Falls, New York, a small group of women had gathered in 1848 for the first woman suffrage convention in America.

From her Christian perspective, Jane too was interested in helping women.[1] She wanted to help them know the loving God Who had a plan for each life, Who created each one as a person of worth and value. Now, at Columbia, she was diligently preparing herself for her new role: woman educator. Her classes with John Dewey, leader in the Progressive Education Movement, stimulated a lot of critical thinking as Jane considered De-

wey's concepts and their possible usefulness to her work in Persia.

Elsewhere in the United States, changes were popping out
everywhere. The first women governors, Nellie Tayloe Ross of
Wyoming and Amanda Ferguson of Texas, were elected. More
women were working away from home as industrial technology
moved society away from its essentially agrarian base. Canned
goods, ready-made clothing and new household appliances were
freeing women from many of their daily housekeeping and farm-
ing responsibilities. Young flappers were shocking their elders
with short skirts, short hair and a bolder use of cosmetics and
cigarettes.

However, despite numerous cross-currents, American life remained fairly stable. Education, religion and science were making impressive progress. Jane and her family had many lively
discussions about these current events and their possible impact
on society. Probably no two cities in the world presented more of
a contrast than the two which claimed Jane's special interest—
New York and Tehran.

From Tehran came descriptions of Reza Shah's assumption of
power in December, 1925, and the establishment of the Pahlavi
Dynasty. Jane wondered about the impact of this regime upon
the people in Persia.

Then a letter dated Feb. 18, 1926, brought news that touched
Jane's life on a deeply personal level. Her beloved friend, Charlotte, had just surprised everyone with the announcement of her
engagement to Herrick Young, a highly respected young UPI
correspondent and American journalist teaching at Alborz College. A flood of emotions stirred within Jane. She was happy for
Charlotte, but she also realized that she would sorely miss their
close companionship. What would it be like to work without
Charlotte? More difficult? Yes. But Jane faced the new challenge
squarely: was her purpose for being in Iran to join a human
friend or to serve her Master?

Jane's two-year stay at home had given her opportunity to attend graduate school and acquire new skills and information on
currently effective educational procedures. Her study at Biblical
Seminary was both reinforcing and illuminating. Her back operation had greatly improved her physical condition. The enjoya-

ble hours with her family and friends had renewed and re-
freshed her culturally and spiritually. Yet, leaving New York for
the second time was more difficult than before. This new assignment was for a term of six years, not three. Now she more fully
understood the problems and challenges of her new career. Further, she was more aware of what these long separations meant
to her aging parents, her brothers and sister.

As she proceeded with packing and the preparations to leave,
another letter from Tehran arrived. This time it was Charlotte's
fiance', Herrick Young, who was sharing with his family and a
few friends, his personal observations of a glittering once-in-a-
lifetime event: Reza Shah's coronation on April 26, 1926. Jane's
family listened with delight as she read about this real-life Persian folk tale. Herrick Young wrote:

> . . . I have felt more than ever that I was walking in the Arabi-
> an Nights the past few days. The day before the coronation, the
> Persians were painting away at the palace (Golestan) at a great
> rate. 500 men worked all night to get things in shape.
>
> Payne, as my photographer, and I were the only Americans be-
> sides the financiers and the diplomats who saw the coronation.
> The Shah put his own emerald and diamond crown upon his
> head, and sat on the real Peacock Throne which has been
> sealed up in the palace for years . . . .

It is said that by the time Reza Khan reached adulthood, he
was still illiterate. But by studying, reading and writing after his
day's army duties were completed, and with the help of others
about him, he succeeded in overcoming this enormous handicap.

The shah was deeply ambitious for his country, one of the
poorest in the world. Only the foreigners who had been granted
the rights to control the country's principal resources were pros-
pering—plus a few of the Iranians within the land who were
supporting these dealings. Corruption, deceit, opium addiction,
superstition, malnutrition, unhygienic conditions, contaminated
water, disease—malaria, typhoid, trachoma, plague, cholera—
and famine were some of the problems in Iran which the new
shah faced.

Ignorance also afflicted the whole of Iran. Less than one percent of the population was literate. There were practically no

schools in Tehran except for the few small private schools such
as Iran Bethel. Women, for the most part, did not go to school
and were deprived of the rights which women in some neighbor-
ing countries had already been granted and were using in behalf
of their countries.

Medically, the infant mortality rate was one of the highest in
the world; and the average life span was only about thirty. Politically, the entrenched mullahs were the dominating ruling power.
Tribal and minority strife kept the people in turmoil. Economi-
cally, poverty was everywhere. The people were handicapped by
unemployment, in part because they lacked adequate tools,
equipment and training. Iran's roads were poor, though it didn't
matter much since there were few automobiles. There were also
no railways. There were, however, a few phones and each was
considered a real luxury.

The shah wondered how Iran could move into the twentieth
century and he sought answers. In 1927 Reza Shah began construction of the Trans-Iranian railroad. When completed, this
linked the Caspian Sea with the Persian Gulf, a matter of great
importance to the country.

During Jane's return voyage to Iran, as on her first trip, her
constant prayer was that she could live in a way that others
would see and know God's love and plan for all.

I need Thee, Oh, I need Thee,
Every hour I need Thee.

Before assuming principalship of Iran Bethel, Jane, now a
more mature young women of 27, would go to Hamadan for a
year of concentrated study of the Persian language. Nairn and
Company had recently established a new fleet of buses that
crossed the desert, and Jane was pleased to discover that Dr. and
Mrs. Samuel Zwemer were traveling on her bus. Dr. Zwemer
was an authority among Christians on Islam and it was a privilege to travel with him. Furthermore, her friend, Dr. William
Wysham of the Persia Mission, had been sent to Beirut to escort
the Zwemers to Tehran.

Years later, Jane would smile at the memory of their travel in
an open car across the desert from Baghdad to Kermanshah, dust
constantly swirling around them:

Dr. Zwemer would stretch his long legs out as far as possible (all of us were well-cramped) and recite "How beautiful upon the mountains are the feet of him that bringeth good tidings, that publishes peace" (Isaiah 52:7). He would chuckle as he glanced at his worn-out, dusty shoes. He had a new and compelling Bible verse for every situation!

As Jane settled in as teacher-student at the Faith Hubbard School for Girls in Hamadan,[2] she was reminded of the Biblical account of Esther, for Hamadan (previously known as Ecbatana)[3] was the location of one of the three palaces from which Esther's husband had ruled. Esther spent a whole year preparing for her presentation to the king, Xerxes (Ahasuerus), and he had chosen her to be his queen. Jane felt that her forthcoming year was, likewise, preparation for service to her King in a role for which she, too, had been chosen.

Jane spent much time wading through a nineteen volume history of Persia in the Persian language.

She was fascinated by the Muslim version of many stories she knew from the Bible. In one of her letters home, she told about the Persian version of Moses:

> In case you don't know why Moses' speech was encumbered, when he was a baby in Pharaoh's household he got a bit playful with Pharaoh and began to pull out the gentleman's whiskers. This did not please Pharaoh, as he thought it inappropriate to his dignity, and as there were other indications that this child was the feared prophet that was to come, his majesty wished to kill the child at once. Trying to disprove this charge of his being a prophet, the household said they would put him to the test to show he was a mere baby. So they put before the young Moses two dishes, one full of reddish fruit—some say rubies—another filled with glowing coals. Moses picked up the coals and put them in his mouth and thereafter could never say the letter "s", it always becoming "th" because of the burn he suffered at that time! However, Pharaoh was convinced and let him live!

Being in Hamadan also brought Daniel, another Old Testament personality, to Jane's mind. According to Biblical history, Daniel was just a young man, a teenage prince, when he was carried off into ancient Persia (Babylon) when Judah was conquered by Nebuchadnezzar, the Gentile king of Babylon. The king want-

ed "children in whom was no blemish, but well favoured and
skillful in all wisdom, and cunning in knowledge, and understanding science, and such as had ability in them to stand in the
king's palace . . ." (Daniel 1:4).

Daniel lived in Babylon through the reigns of Kings Nebuchadnezzar and Belshazzar, and the conquest of the Medes and
Persians. In all this time, Daniel never wavered in worshipping
the God of heaven, however, and this was known to the other
leaders in the kingdom. When King Darius, the Persian, took the
kingdom, Daniel was made prime minister over the greatest empire in antiquity, and some of Daniel's enemies plotted to get
him out of the way. They tricked Darius into signing a decree
that no one could pray or petition any god or man other than
Darius himself. As expected, this did not stop Daniel from his
daily prayers to God. Consequently, he was arrested and thrown
in the lions' den, much to King Darius' consternation. However,
when the king rushed to the lions' den the next morning to see if
Daniel's God had delivered him, he found Daniel alive and well.
The king was so happy that he issued another decree:

> That in every dominion of my kingdom men tremble and fear
> before the God of Daniel: for he is the living God, and steadfast
> forever, and his kingdom that which shall not be destroyed,
> and his dominion shall be even unto the end (Daniel 6:26).

In pondering this story, Jane hoped that her faithfulness to
God would be such that the students she would be leading
would know that her God "is the living God, and . . . His kingdom that which shall not be destroyed."

Hamadan itself, Jane was learning, was an illustrious and ancient city located on the old "silk route" used by Marco Polo on
his journey through Persia. Hamadan was also the setting where
many past kingdoms were destroyed. Cyrus made the city
(called Hagmatana, which the Greeks translated into Ecbatana)
the summer capitol of his empire. At 6000 feet above sea level,
Hamadan is cool in summer and very cold in the winter; Mount
Alvand, more than 11,000 feet high, stands nearby.[4] When Darius became king, he kept Ecbatana as a summer palace.

It was the usual custom for Persian kings, together with an
enormous entourage, to make seasonal journeys over the land.
They would travel between the winter palace at Susa, to Persepo-

lis[5] in the spring, and Ecbatana in summer. In doing so, they crossed more than 800 miles of rugged high mountains and flat, arid terrain. Over the centuries, Ecbatana had been invaded, occupied and destroyed by enemies numerous times. Each time, the survivors of such catastrophes regrouped and carried on. Jane now understood why the cypress is the symbolic art form which expresses the Iranians' ability to endure and adapt to change—the cypress steadfastly clings to its roots despite the winds and storms which batter and bend it low.

Archaeologists have long wanted to undertake extensive excavation in this multi-layered region. What ancient artifacts and treasures lie packed beneath the surface: Xerxes treasury? Alexander's loot from Persepolis? But the living, active presence of Hamadan interferes with digging into the somnolent past of Ecbatana. Sometimes when Jane would walk through Hamadan, she'd look down at her two small, black-laced shoes moving over the dusty earth and wonder if she were an intruding presence in a strategy session of kings, warriors, conquerors and slaves?

While Jane was an eager learner, some of the lessons from her stay in Hamadan proved very difficult. Also, Jane discovered that she and her faculty associate did not see eye-to-eye. In summer, Jane's language teacher, a Muslim, met with her in the garden at 5:00 each morning for her lesson. But in winter the teacher would arrive before sun-up, just prior to the first Muslim prayer time. When that time came, the turbaned, long-robed teacher would politely ask to be excused while he said his prayers. Jane would leave the room in order that he could have time and privacy for his devotions. "I'm glad he takes time to acknowledge God," she reasoned. However, upon hearing of this arrangement, her housemate, the principal, strenuously objected to having a Muslim pray in her living room.

Another time, a young orphan girl, who was given board and lodging in exchange for cooking and housework, was shown how to cook liver. However, when liver was again on the menu three weeks later, the poor girl had forgotten how to cook it. The teenager was severely reprimanded and sought refuge in Jane's room where she remained until transferred to Kermanshah to be with other Urumia orphans.

Such incidents distressed Jane. She wondered what she would

do if she were in charge? She had learned that exactness and excellence were essential, both from her father, a chemical engineer and inventor, and from her own chemistry major in college. "But," she concluded, "one also needs to allow for time and patience."

One noon, just as she was dismissing the classes, she received word that visitors were awaiting her. Jane hurried across the grounds to the living room trying to guess who in the world was there? She was delighted to see her friends, the Markers, with whom she had first come to Persia. Her parents had frequently heard Jane tell about the adventures she shared with this young couple who had been assigned to Hamadan.

After a few initial pleasantries, Merrell Marker said, "Jane, do you have a brother?"

"Yes, two brothers," Jane replied with a sudden sense of anxiety.

Merrell continued. "We have received a cable from your parents: 'Tell Jane Nathaniel died this morning cause infantile paralysis.'"

Jane was stunned! She couldn't believe it. Her little brother Nat; so bright, with such a promising future, and just back from his summer tour of Europe. He had been all eager to return to Rutgers for his sophomore year. At twenty-one, he was the joy of life to his family.

Merrell asked quietly, "Would you like to send a cable in reply? If so, we'll take it to the telegraph office right now."

Jane nodded her head. "Thank you. Please excuse me for a few minutes while I write it."

Eleanor clasped Jane's hand, "Don't hurry. We'll wait right here."

Upstairs in her room, Jane quickly wrote two Scripture references. Her family would understand—it was through their love that she had learned the meaning of these passages. "The eternal God is thy refuge, and underneath are the everlasting   arms . . . " (Deuteronomy 33:27). ". . . But my God shall supply all your need according to his riches in glory by Christ Jesus" (Philippians 4:19).

Jane gave the Markers her message and walked to the door with her friends. At the bottom of the stairs, they waved to her.

Jane waved back before quietly closing the door. She walked straight up to her room. She was in a daze. She sat erect, lost in the pain of her thoughts. Suddenly, she remembered that there was a faculty meeting scheduled for today. Jane rose, washed her face, brushed her hair and joined the other teachers in the staff room. In seconds, she realized that they, too, had been given the news. She deeply appreciated their silent sympathy.

Nat's death was the first break in the circle of Jane's immediate family. "I will not leave you comfortless.... I will come to you" (John 14:18) was a promise she had learned as a child. And indeed, the Spirit of God did bring her comfort as she invited the Master to help her, and her family, in this time of grief and separation. Since it took about three months for a letter to travel between the United States and Iran, Jane knew she'd have to wait a long time before hearing the details from home. However, she wrote to her parents at once, finding great comfort in thinking about them and their deep faith and commitment.

Next morning, Jane was up at 5:00 A.M. for her regular language lesson. As her father had often remarked, "Life must go on—mourning and distressing others will not change the situation." Jane reflected how,when she was a teenager, the death of one of her schoolmates had impressed her with the uncertainty of life. Then and there she had decided it was necessary to live each day to the best of one's ability and Jane had undertaken to improve the quality of her life. Each week she had selected an ideal or virtue that she wanted to develop or strengthen. On her mirror she had tucked a small card, bearing a word or two to remind her of this ideal. Now, Jane studied her Bible with new zeal and purpose, to remind herself of how God answered people's needs in time of crisis and challenge.

To Jane's surprise and delight, Charlotte appeared from Tehran that same week to spend a few days with her. Charlotte had lost her own dear youngest brother and understood Jane's pain only too well. They shared precious hours together, and then, too soon, Charlotte was gone.

Jane often thought of Charlotte in Tehran, and through correspondence maintained her friendship, though separated by many miles. Charlotte was helping get things ready for Jane's return to Iran Bethel:

Faith Hubbard School
Hamadan, Persia
April 9, 1927

Dear Sharley:

It was so good to receive your letter this afternoon! I have been fighting specific devils lately and also remembering very vividly all the days just a year ago [when she returned to Persia and began study at Hamadan] besides getting letters from mother . . . so I needed something warming. I need to get out, but a nice storm seems imminent.

You may expect practically all of my junk most any time after the 20th of this month, as George is coming through then and will take it up for me. If you would dump it into the Boarding cellar, though don't smash the dishes. Did you get the key I sent? I'll be glad to get all out of the way before the weather gets hot. I'll send any other keys and instructions necessary for rugs to unpack and put on the floor there for me, for I feel if that cellar is just a wee bit fixed up with my junk when I arrive, I will feel I have some place and it won't give me the desperation that being in Ingleside would. Thank you . . . .

So sorry to know you are having so much typhoid. Here's hoping none of you get it. Smallpox has been the rage here . . . .

About my coming up in June, are some actions being taken or letters written from Tehran as I asked Lillian? Otherwise I have to leave as early as the 11th, though goodness knows the time will be short enough then. Time is rushing on much too fast for me at this end, too, and I shall have to leave all these good friends . . . .

Why did you remember my birthday, dear? Thank you heaps for thinking of it. I think some records will be great but you shouldn't have done it! . . . .

I did write home about your staying there while studying in N.Y.—but Mother is not at all well so Dad may sit on the idea at once, and I know you will understand, therefore, if you do not hear from them. If they do consider it, I think you could do heaps for them for it is a lonely household with loads of space to jiggle around in. Each letter from Catherine is more bitter than the last. Do pray for her.

Am trying to go full tilt on 3rd year language study while the going is good . . . .

The poem I like best this week is:

I could not keep on with the fight,
I could not face my want, my sin,
The baffled hope, the urgent foe,
The mighty wrong, the struggle right,
Excepting that I surely know,
Sometime—sometime—
Some dear time, I shall win.

There is so much to rejoice about, isn't there?

Best love to you always,
Jane

June 2, 1927 is the date on Jane's last letter from Hamadan to Charlotte. Charlotte had just left Tehran and was on her way to the U.S.A. for her wedding.

Sharley Darling:

A letter from my beloved mother this afternoon asked me to be sure and tell her when you would arrive so they could see you before you left for Bucyrus. I have just written her and told her I have sent her every bit of me that is humanly possible through you who have meant the world to me here. Oh, I don't know Sharley—it has made me so desperately homesick starting you off—I could just lie down and cry and cry and cry for my mother and all, for my little brother . . . only as sure as I do there comes a knock at my door and I must flee.

I have been thinking of you today starting across the desert—and as I took the girls for a swim before a call and church I wished I might give you some of the coldness of it. My prayers have been with you more than constantly.

By the time you get this you'll be happy and thrilled, but that first part of the trip is taxing. I have thought so many times of how lovely and up-to-date you looked as you started out! Not at all as I did, with my wretched old clothes . . . you don't need to worry about your appearance one little bit.

Dear old Ysme is busy bringing water for me to wash my hair—having just finished a good job of taking a terrible tea stain from my coat. I shall miss her in Tehran for she surely is a good old soul.

And now the wee moon is so glorious: I am wondering if you saw it on the Tigris last night and if you are revelling in the glory of the desert tonight. Is anything more peaceful and vast! I loved traveling under the stars. Wonder if you travel by night or rest? I preferred to get there!

It is Friday nowonly three more days of school—and then I must really begin work. If I could only get a bit of rest in-between, but it looks sort of hopeless. It will be good to be at the Bentley's tonight—they are so fine—and then the Funk's tomorrow.

I love this poem:

Father,
Make me, keep me
Thy child this day:
Make me simple and loyal,
Loving and true
As a child.
Teach me to look unto thee
Like a child's unquestioning trust in his father,
Teach me to look unto thee
With a child's simple pride in his father's strength and wisdom
    and skill,
Teach me, O Father,
Every moment I live to depend upon thee like a child
Make me, keep me,
Thy child this day.

Read it to yourself in the solemn hush of the Milan Cathedral—when a choir is singing softly—and know it is my prayer for you and for me.

This will doubtless be your last letter from me till you reach Paris and Ricky—and there may your joy be complete.

Ever devotedly,
Jane

NOTES

1. Jane's concern for women may also have been influenced by her second cousin, Jane Addams (1860-1935), an American social worker and humanitarian who founded Hull House in Chicago. In 1931 she shared the Nobel Peace Prize with Nicholas Murray Butler, President of Columbia University. She sponsored a number of reforms, including the first eight-hour law for working women, the first state child-labor law, housing reforms and the first juvenile court. She had planned to become a physician but was prevented from doing so by her health.

2. The Faith Hubbard School in Hamadan was begun on October 25, 1882 and, at first, included both boys and girls. Financial gifts from Miss Faith Hubbard of the Women's Board of New York, and Mrs. Sherwood, mother of one of the young women teachers on the school's staff, provided funds for the construction of a new building. It opened in 1885 as Faith Hubbard School with an enrollment of about eighty-five pupils. In 1927, the school provided adult education programs which missionaries attended in order to gain or enhance their mastery of the Persian language.

3. Ecbatana was sacked by Alexander the Great in 333 B.C.

4. Jane once made the climb up Mount Alvand to 11,000 feet but could go no further.

5. Persepolis was built for ceremonial celebrations, including the "No Ruz" (New Year's) rites.

Part II

Share With Me the Iranian Dream

CHAPTER FIVE

Learning by Doing

When Jane reached Tehran (1927) to assume
her new duties as principal of Iran Bethel, she plunged right into her new career. In one of her last letters to Charlotte, Jane had included a prayer which she said was "the poem for the day on which I take over the school. May I never forget it!"

God let me be aware,
Let me not stumble blindly down the ways,
Just getting somehow safely through the days,
Not even wondering why it all was planned—
Eyes to the ground, unseeking for the light,
Soul never aching for a wild-winged flight.
Please, keep me eager just to do my share.
God—let me be aware.
God—let me be aware.
Stab my soul fiercely with other's pains.
Let me walk seeing horror and stain.
Let my hands, groping, find other hands.
Give me the courage, wounded, to fight;
Flood me with knowledge, drench me with light.
Please, keep me eager just to do my share.
God—let me be aware.

When Jane had first arrived at Iran Bethel, it was a growing school. Now, all of Jane's former Ingleside housemates were gone: Miss Peet was home on furlough; Lillian McHenry had resigned as president to become the wife of the highly respected clergyman, Dr. Henry C. Shuler; Charlotte Young was married to Herrick Young and living elsewhere in Tehran. The current, highly competent staff included an American, ten to fifteen Iranian teachers and a number of college-educated missionary wives. There were some 200-300 students from primary grades through high school, and the number was constantly increasing. Many of the girls were Armenian, but more Muslim girls were enrolling because of the school's fine academic program and its high moral and ethical standards.

People noticed a big change in Jane. Dr. Wysham recalls that when Jane was at Iran Bethel the first time, she was rather quiet and followed all her instructions carefully and cooperatively. But:

> When she came back the second time, believe me, she was ready to take off! She knew what she was doing and how to do it. She had the education, a heart of love, and real concern and compassion for the Iranians. Her girls received new insights. Following in her example, many of them set out to help others. They developed their abilities and some of them later assumed important leadership roles. Most of these women loved their country deeply and wanted to serve and help it become a better place for all the people. Jane Doolittle was highly respected and admired for her life of selfless dedication and service to both the rich and the poor.

As always when registering at Iran Bethel, students and parents were informed of the rules and regulations. These included the facts that it was a Christian school, that there would be Christian prayers, and that the girls were expected to be in regular attendance. Then the parents were given an agreement to sign. The Muslim students were intrigued by the fact that Christian prayers seemed unmemorized, very personal, and rather informal and conversational in nature. In contrast, when they prayed to Allah they used the Arabic prayers found in the Quran which few understood. The school's curriculum included studies in English, science, math, history, geography, physical education (in the form of games and play at recess), singing, music (piano), Bible and daily chapel.

After years of no boarders at the school, a new dormitory had been opened in an old building in the northeast corner of the Central Mission Compound while Jane was in America (1924-1926). During the dorm's first year, it was occupied by one student and one matron, an elderly former Muslim who had become a Christian, with Charlotte serving as supervisor. More live-in students were added the following year. Jane took up residence in this dormitory, and soon there were some twenty students, plus staff, overcrowding the building. One of Jane's new responsibilities as principal was to over-see the construction of a larger dorm. It would be the first building on the Sage College property which was located just two blocks south of the Alborz College property.[1] In February, 1929, there was great rejoicing when a fine new sixty-bed dorm was ready for occupancy. Now girls from throughout Iran could live on campus. Soon this dorm was fully occupied and, with other teachers living there, Jane was able to move from the dorm to another building. One of the Assyrian students remembers coming to the school about this time:

... In September, 1929, I went from Tabriz to attend the Presbyterian Mission's Girls' High School in Tehran. Miss Doolittle was principal. She also lived in and administered the boarding division where I lived for three years. To my knowledge this was the only high school for girls in the country ....

Travel was not easy. Roads were centuries old, mostly just camel caravan dirt roads winding through treacherous mountain passes. It took three days of day and night driving to get to Tehran. There were no hotels or motels on the way.

A Russian-born Iranian from Tabriz, a Turkish Armenian girl, . . . and I were the only ones who did not veil. Somehow we stood out!

Upon graduation I returned to Tabriz for three years of teaching. Then I went on to the American University of Beirut to study nursing. I was well established there on the staff of the university when war came along and I had to return to Iran . . . I worked in Mashad Mission Hospital for two years when I was asked to go to Tehran and plan, open and administer a military hospital for the U.S. Army until the arrival of a medical unit . . . .

All through these years I have maintained my contact with Miss Doolittle, as have all her students—we admired and loved her . . . . In the example of her life and service, she raised the aspirations and social consciousness of her students . . . . It was her students who initiated, backed, pushed and saw the 1975 Family Protection Act passed.

Another of Jane's varied responsibilities as principal included the hiring of help. When a cook was needed in the dormitory,Golebehar came into Jane's life. In the years ahead, Golebehar would become very special to her. When Golebehar, meaning "Spring Flower", was only four years old, she and some other children were playing in the street of her village (probably in Arabia), when a man approached and told them to follow him. The next thing she knew, all six children were slaves in a home in Tehran. Golebehar always wondered about her mother—what did she do when her little girl did not come home?

Such slaves were generally well cared for in Iran, and Golebehar was treated as one of the family. When she was still young, she was married to another slave in the same household. They had three children, two boys and a girl. When their master died, the slaves were freed, and that was when Golebehar came to Iran Bethel to work. She brought with her Mahmoud, her youngest son, then ten years old. He was crippled by "water on the knee" which had not been properly cared for, and he used a cane or crutch. His mother called him her "grasshopper" as she watched him jump around with his cane. Golebehar herself was a rather tall, slender, very black woman with kinky hair. She was a devout Muslim who had a heart full of love for her work and the girls at Iran Bethel. "So much wisdom, so full of fun," said one of the girls. She was also devoted to her "Khanum" Doolittle.

As principal, Jane attended all kinds of meetings, planning sessions and conferences. It was at one of these gatherings for Christians that Jane met Gertrude, a young Armenian-Jewess who would become a lifelong friend. Gertrude Margaret Norollah (meaning "Light of God") was connected to the life of Iran Bethel in many ways. Born in Tehran in 1897, she traced her family roots back to the time of King Cyrus, when the King's decree enabled all Jews then exiled in Babylon to return to Jerusalem. Gertrude's ancestors had chosen to remain in Persia. Many of her paternal forbears served as court physicians, and her grandfather had been a doctor.

One day, a missionary from the Churches Ministry Among the Jews (CMJ) called upon Gertrude's grandfather and left a copy of the Gospel in Persian for the family to read. One of his sons read it later on and was touched by the words. He accepted

the Way, the Truth and the Life of Jesus Christ, and was baptized
by Dr. Potter at the American Mission after studying with him.
The young convert then went to England, located the CMJ head-
quarters, enrolled in school and trained to become a missionary.
When he returned to Tehran, he wanted to marry a Christian girl
and was introduced to Esther, one of the Iran Bethel students.
They were married and Gertrude was the third of their daughters.

Gertrude and her sisters were educated in England. She returned to Tehran in 1924 after being graduated from London
University's St. Katherine's Teachers' Training College. She
would serve for forty years as headmistress of a girls' school
founded by her father. Many of the school's graduates went on
to Iran Bethel for further study.

Gertrude's mother, Esther, had been a student at Iran Bethel
on the day that Nasser-al-din Shah, the Qajar ruling king (1848-
1896), came to school on an unexpected inspection tour. He was
trying to find out if any Muslim girls were attending which was
strictly forbidden at that time. The students had gathered in the
assembly hall. When he came in, the shah saw an organ and
asked if one of the students would play for him. All of the girls
were so awed that none of them volunteered. However, since
one does not keep a king waiting, the principal had called upon
Esther to play. With great trepidation, thirteen year old Esther
had gone to the organ. When she was finished, the shah had expressed his delight.

He had then asked to have some of the girls write on the
blackboard. One child had taken the chalk, but was too nervous
to write. The shah took the chalk from her hand and wrote on the
board in French and Persian that "the Minister of the Court had
visited there that day." (The school framed his writing on the
blackboard and it remained until the school was abandoned
when Damavand College removed it.) Impressed by the work of
the school, the shah had made a financial contribution to it for
several years thereafter.

Wells College continued sending teachers to Iran Bethel, and
in 1928 Charlotte Stone came to spend a year. She came to complete the usual three-year term of Helen Rose who had left early
to marry. Charlotte explains:

Jane was my boss, and it was my first experience of employment of any kind. My affection and admiration of Jane was great. She had already mastered the language and was so efficient and dedicated to her work. As I naturally felt rather "shaky" in my new venture, I appreciated her patience and humor . . . . I recall the regular meetings in her office when she taught her staff the fundamentals of good teaching. And I recall her studying while sitting on cushions on the floor, her feet under the "coorsie"[2] to keep warm, reading by the light of a kerosene lamp.

A prominent Christian physician, Dr. Sa'eed,[3] lived near the school compound. His young son, Samuel, a well-educated, distinguished engineer, wooed and won Charlotte Stone. They subsequently shared forty-six happy years of marriage.

Marjorie Palmer came from America to Iran Bethel as a permanent staff member and served between 1928 and 1933. Jane assigned Marjorie the task of supervising the school's annual Christmas celebration, as one of her tasks. Marjorie recalls:

I was pleased with the prospects when an opportunity came for a trip to Isfahan. A young Persian, a great friend of all the missionaries, invited Charlotte Stone and me to accompany him south where we would be guests in the home of the manager of the British Bank and his family. He would make all the arrangements for transportation, (which was no small thing in those years). I realized my first responsibility was to Jane and to the project she had assigned to me. I went to her to explain our invitation. She graciously excused me from the assignment and we spent the Christmas holiday vacation on the only trip to Isfahan I had during my five years in Iran.

Such actions were typical of Jane. As an educational administrator she considered it important that her teachers be happy in their service. (On Jane's next furlough, Marjorie would serve as principal.)

In 1929, Margaret Brown, the last Wells-supported graduate, arrived:

. . . The bottom of the market had dropped out; and also, much to my consternation, the hemlines had also dropped—for me and my three-years' supply of dresses! But Jane's calm approach to such things, and her acceptance of me from the outset, made my hemlines inconsequential. As I look back, one of

Jane's outstanding traits was her total acceptance of everyone. I recall no time when she ever said to me "Had you thought?" or "Don't you think?" or "Why don't you . . . ?" And there must have been occasional provocations for such.

In all Jane's relationships there was a friendliness, a warmth, and a great dignity. Her dignity did not preclude fun times: tea-time at the school after classes or at a Lalezar cafe, social activities with fellowmen and new-found friends, and our [school] children and their parents; relaxed and giggly times over stories, trips, reminiscences; quiet times, mission meetings, prayers, chapels; and winter-night times, sitting under our coorsie to keep warm, to study and just to visit. It was a full life and Jane helped make it so . . . .

. . . I sensed strongly Jane's deep devotion to being a good emissary of the Lord Jesus in the land to which she had chosen to go . . . . I vividly remember she took time off one afternoon to come over to my room in Sage compound to visit . . . to try to inculcate in me that wonderful opportunity, as she saw it, of being a vibrant messenger of the Lord.

While Jane did her best to help create and maintain a friendly supportive environment for all her associates, she was always, from the moment of her arrival in Persia, eager to know and understand the culture and mores of the country. The Iranians received her cordially and with kindness for she was always pleased to be included in their celebrations and to experience their customs. While Jane had studied in Hamadan, she had been privileged to participate in one of the most significant Muslim traditions—"Ramazan," or "Ramadan," the month of fasting.[4] The Ramazan fast (from food, drink, smoking and sex during the daylight hours) is one of the five pillars of Islam. These include the profession of faith that Allah is one God and Muhammad is his prophet, the five daily prayers, alms giving, and, if humanly possible, at least one pilgrimage to Mecca in a lifetime.

Ramazan is the ninth month in the Muslim lunar calendar. The fast celebrates Muhammad's month of fasting in a cave near Mecca fourteen centuries ago. According to Islam, it was then that Allah designated Muhammad as his prophet to the Arabs and began to reveal the Quran, the Muslim holy book.

During Ramazan, non-Muslims and foreigners residing in a Muslim country must abide by the fasting regulations in public.

Failure to do so can result in a fine, possible imprisonment, or both. However, the very young, the very old, the sick, travelers, nursing mothers and the mentally incompetent are exempted. The sick are required to make up the missed fasting days when they get well, and those who cannot abstain are required to feed a poor or needy person.

> O believers, prescribed for you is the Fast, even as it was pre-scribed for those that were before you—haply you will be god-fearing—for days numbered: and if any of you be sick, or if he be on a journey, then a number of other days; and for those who are able to fast, a redemption by the feeding of a poor man. Yet better it is for him who volunteers good, and that you should fast is better for you, if you but know; the month of Ramazan, wherein the Quran was sent down to be a guidance to the people, and as clear signs of the Guidance and the Salva-tion. So let those of you, who are present at the month, fast it; and if any of you be sick, or if he be on a journey, then a num-ber of other days; God desires ease for you, and desires not hardship for you; and that you fulfill the number, and magnify God that He has guided you, and haply you will be thankful.
> (Sura 2:183-185)[5]

Early in her time in Iran, one of Jane's students invited Jane to join her and her family in a nearby village for a few days during Ramazan. On the appointed day, Soqra brought Jane by carriage and donkey to her home, arriving shortly after the 6:30 evening gun sounded to indicate sundown.[6] Jane joined the female mem-bers of the family and the other women guests to share the even-ing meal of rice, chicken, greens, cheese and bread. About 11:30 p.m. the guests departed and Jane and the family retired. The family slept in their usual places under the coorsie but Jane was given a small room to herself where she slept on a mattress near a small lighted fire.

At 3:30 a.m., Soqra woke Jane for the next meal, one much like that of the preceding evening. The women and girls seated them-selves at the table to eat, then gathered around the coorsie to drink tea. At 4:30 a.m. a gun sounded, signifying that there would be no more food or drink until sundown. No one would go back to sleep until after the evening meal.

"Soqra, since this ritual doesn't mean too much to you, why

do you participate in it?" Jane asked, trying to understand the culture and customs.

"Because," Soqra explained, "it upsets our mother if we do not obey. I do it to please her." As the first wife who had born only daughters, Soqra's mother had been pushed aside in favor of a new and younger wife whom the husband hoped would bear sons.

Jane marveled at the patience of Soqra's mother for she had to awaken the servants in time to prepare the 3:30 A.M. meal. As a concerned mother, she tried to insure that her children ate enough food to sustain them through their entire school day. However, many students' school work often suffered during the month of fasting.

"Moharram" is another month-long Muslim observance. It commemorates the Shi'ite martyrs who died for their belief in Allah. During Moharram three men are especially mourned for their martyrdom: Ali, son-in-law and cousin of Muhammad, and his two sons, Hassan and Hussein. One dramatic highpoint of Moharram occurs on "Ashura," the tenth day of the month when Hussein and seventy-three of his followers were brutally massacred at Karbala. During Ashura, hundreds of men, stripped to the waist, march in the streets while flagellating themselves with chains and swords, performing ritual dances and calling out the names of Hussein and his retinue.[7]

In contrast to these celebrations of mourning and fasting, Jane also learned about "No Ruz" (New Day),[8] a joyful Persian celebration commencing on the vernal equinox (March 21). No Ruz marks the coming of spring and the beginning of the new year in the Persian solar calendar.[9] Fifteen days before No Ruz, people plant wheat seeds or lentils in a shallow bowl, and the growing green shoots symbolize the coming of spring. Meanwhile, the women in the family are busy giving their dwelling a thorough cleaning. If possible, new furnishings, curtains or other items are purchased, and every member of the family receives new clothes and shoes.

For No Ruz, the "Haft Sin" table is set with seven items which all begin with the letter "s". These include "sabzi" (greens), "sib" (apples), "sekeh" (coins), "sonbol" (hyacinth), "somagh" (sumac), "sir" (garlic) and "samanou" (a Persian halva). The table is also laid with a mirror between candles, a Quran, unleavened bread, colored eggs, fruits, nuts, candy and goldfish in a bowl. Some families also include a leaf floating in a small glass container, since it is believed that the leaf will move slightly at the exact moment when the sun crosses the equator.

People visit in each other's homes throughout the thirteen-day holiday. Sometimes people exchange gifts, but more often the older, richer and more important people give gold or silver coins to children and to their younger employees. Workers generally receive a bonus of month's wages. On "Seezdah No Ruz", the thirteenth day, all the green shoots planted for the occasion must be thrown into running water, and people spend the day outside exulting in the beauties of nature.

During Jane's No Ruz visits, she met many of the student's female relatives. As soon as she entered the house, tea would be served with fruit, sweets and nuts. If she had been invited for dinner, a "sofreh" (cloth) would be spread on the beautifully carpeted floor and covered with large plates and bowls of food, such as bread, rice, vegetables, lamb or chicken, greens, cheese and sauces. Guests begin eating at once, not waiting for anyone else, and with little conversation, since everyone is totally absorbed in eating. The meal concludes with a dessert followed by bowls piled high with different varieties of fruit.

Jane remembers looking forward eagerly to participating in her first No Ruz. The Iran Bethel girls had all tried to explain "Chahar Shahbeh Souri", the good luck ritual that takes place on the last Tuesday before No Ruz.

"You jump over fire, Miss Doolittle!", Shahnaz had said with an impish smile.

"What on earth for?", Jane had asked with curiosity. All the girls had started to talk at once.

"Just a minute, please," Jane had interrupted, "I can really listen to only one of you at a time. Shahnaz started, let her finish, then you'll all have a turn."

With a look of satisfaction, Shahnaz had continued. "You jump over the fire to get past the past; to wipe out bad troubles, sickness, disappointments—whatever you don't like—and you make a wish for good fortune for the new year. It's a very old tradition and it brings good luck." Shahnaz felt she'd done a good job with her explanation and she smiled.

"You leave on your long skirts, your chadors, and jump over a fire?" Jane had asked with exaggerated skepticism.

The girls had burst out laughing and Jane had laughed with them. Finally, Assieh thought it time to stop the hilarity. "Stop it," she said, mimicking Jane's mannerisms, "that is enough. Miss Doolittle will come to my house. My aunt speaks English and will explain it properly!"

Shahnaz had protested loudly. "No, Assieh, she comes to my house. My father is more important than yours!"

"Shades of human nature!" Jane thought. Shahnaz's assertion reminded her of a story her Aunt Laura had told. Her aunt had been listening as the other girls in her exclusive school were bragging about their father's importance. Laura's father was one of the most successful steel manufacturers in the east. His factory produced ingots called "pigs", and Aunt Laura had mischievously said, "My father sells pigs!" Misunderstanding, the other girls had been horrified and had snubbed her the rest of the day.

"Every person, anywhere in the world, wants to feel special," mused Jane as she compared these behaviors.

It had finally worked out that Jane accepted Assieh's invitation and visited Shahnaz later. In the early evening, Jane gathered with the rest of Assieh's family in the garden. A small, two-foot square, heap of camel thorn twigs and brush was piled together and set afire. One by one, each family member leaped over the small flames while the others stood around clapping and cheering.

Amid encouraging words and expectant smiles, Jane had taken her turn in jumping. When she finished, the family felt that Jane was one of them now! Assieh and her mother rushed to Jane's side. Jane said to Assieh, "Please tell your mother that I thank you all for having invited me here tonight, and that I look forward to the day when I can speak to her in Persian and express my appreciation directly." Then she had bowed and smiled. For Jane, learning by doing was the best learning of all!

NOTES

1. A book written in the early 1900s by a distinguished woman educator, Anna Garlin Spencer, entitled *Women's Share in Social Culture,*

brought public attention to the need for women's participation in broader cultural activities. The foundation established from the fortune of
Russell Sage (related to Jane's paternal grandmother) was headed by his
wife, Margaret Olivia Slocum Sage. She provided vast sums for the improvement of social and living conditions. In 1924-25, during the time
that Jane was home, arrangements were made with the Sage Endow-
ment to provide funds to begin the development of higher education for
women in Iran. When Jane returned to Tehran in 1927, the property for
Sage College for Women was purchased. With the assistance of a distinguished Iranian architect and the cooperation of a committee from the
U.S. Presbyterian Board of Foreign Missions in New York, Jane was involved in the construction of this school. It was to be an extension of the
educational program for Iran Bethel girls who wished to continue education in their own homeland. Government schools continued to the
eleventh grade only. Iran Bethel had always offered a twelfth grade, so
now they offered a thirteenth and began a Junior College. It was hoped
that Sage College would one day be accredited as a four-year college for
women. The new building was ready for occupancy in 1929.

   2. A "coorsie" is a low-standing table about three to four feet square.
Under it is placed a brazier of burning charcoal covered with its ashes so
the fire will smoulder for twenty-four hours. Thin mattresses to sit on
are placed on all four sides, as well as cushions at the back to lean upon.
The family sits with their legs under the table, being careful not to get
their feet—whose shoes have been removed—in the fire. Thus, the body
from the waist down is beautifully warmed, making the whole body feel
warm.

   3. Dr. Sa'eed Khan Kordestani was a Kord reared in all the traditions
of Islam. Then he met Christ and became one of the outstanding Christians of the country. As he practiced his skills as a physician, he constantly shared the Gospel wherever he went.

   4. Ramazan is observed today by some 900 million Muslims in various parts of the world.

   5. Quoted in *Islam*, edited by John Alden Williams and Georges Braill-
er, p. 45.

   6. "The time of fasting is from the time of night when a white thread
can be distinguished Learning By Doing 97 from a black one . . . until
the sun has fully set below the horizon in the evening." Ibid., page 4.

   7. Reza Shah considered such Ashura actions to be negative. He did
not want the people to use their energies in this way, but to harness
them for positive purposes. Therefore, he began to suppress the more
emotional aspects of the "tazieh", passion plays, which were enacted in
villages during Moharram. These plays depict episodes from Hussein's

life. Some scenes are imaginary, but the central themes always involve persecution, cruelty, mourning and grief. Often those watching the plays become hysterical.

8. Although "No Ruz" is of uncertain origin, it was celebrated in Aechamenian times (553-330 B.C.) and became an integral part of the Zoroastrian religion. King Darius and his son, King Xerxes (Queen Esther's husband), doubtless built Persepolis explicitly for the celebration of these spring rites. During No Ruz, representatives of all nations subject to the king of the Persian Empire, the "King of Kings," would bring to him gifts characteristic of some outstanding feature or product of their particular country. Ferdowsi, the great tenth-century epic poet, and Omar Khayyam (scientist, astronomer, mathematician and poet of the same century) and others have written in detail about this purely Iranian festival. When the Arab Muslims came into Persia in the seventh century, No Ruz is one of the many customs they maintained and celebrated.

9. The Persians lived by two calendars, the solar and the lunar. Since No Ruz is according to the solar calendar, the dates fall at regular times and seasons. The Islamic calendar, their religious calendar, is lunar, however, and all the dates go back ten days each year. Thus, religious seasons fall according to no set date. For example, Moharram and Ramazan may be celebrated in August one year and in October some years later.

CHAPTER SIX

Changing With the Times

In 1931 Jane finished a six-year term. It had been a period of learning, growing and changing, as well as affirming her call to Persia. Now it was time to go home.[1] Jane was eager to see her family. She was also curious to learn what her final grades from Wells had been, for it was Wells' custom to withhold for ten years the final grades for all graduates. Jane had been graduated in 1921. She wondered what marks Dr. Hickok had given her? She also wanted to consult with Dr. Hibbs again, but she hoped that more surgery would not be necessary.

As she contemplated returning to the U.S., Jane thought about the many changes that had taken place in her home: Nat had died; both Catherine and Jed had married and moved to homes of their own. What would her family and home be like now? She knew God would be there, but Nat, especially, would not be. He was now in his heavenly home—without pain, suffering and disappointment.

Jane's homeward journey took her to Quebec, where her family came to meet her. Catherine brought her husband, Howard, whom Jane had previously known; and Jed introduced his beautiful wife, Molly. After a time of rejoicing and visiting, the two young couples left for their respective homes in New York while Jane and her parents began a leisurely trip. They went down the Saguenay River and through Newfoundland and the historic Evangeline Country.

While they traveled they talked of the many changes taking place in the United States. President Hoover was desperately trying to halt the floodtide of depression overruning the country since the stock market crash of '29. In the midst of his heavy responsibilities, he had signed the act making "The Star Spangled Banner" America's national anthem.

Once again welcomed into the warm fellowship of the Doolittle family home, Jane busied herself at Columbia University, continuing to advance her skills and insights in education. Dr. Hibbs was in town—a miracle in itself considering his demanding schedule. He greeted her cordially; undertook thorough examinations; and said, yes, she would need further surgery for the removal of the growth of excess cartilage. They set a date for the operation. While recuperating at home after the operation, Jane continued to read and study.

All too quickly, the time at home with her family passed, and again Jane returned to Iran Bethel. What a time to be in Iran! The shah was vigorously and systematically planting seeds of great change. Anything that Reza Shah did or attempted to do affected everyone in the country, including Jane and her work.

At the first chapel after her return, the students flocked noisily into the room. Jane nodded in recognition to the girls she knew and acknowledged the new students with a special bow. "What a lively, bright group of students!" she thought, "I am glad to be back." After a brief welcome and time of meditation, Jane dismissed the girls to their classes.

The other faculty wondered if Jane had yet learned of the shah's recent decree to end the enrollment of Persian children in all primary schools run by foreigners. However, news of this change had reached Jane at Kermanshah during her return trip. The new decree would mean that about three-fourths of the enrollment at mission schools, including Iran Bethel, would be eliminated. Now, in their first staff meeting, Jane calmly faced the teachers. "You've all carried on so well during my absence," she said, pausing to look into each face. "Now, we must cooperate with the government in its recent ruling. We will do our best to carry on as the Lord leads. I am sorry to say," she said softly, hesitating a moment, "we shall have to drop some of the elementary teachers." Just whom to drop would be a heartache for Jane and the teachers involved.

The takeover of the primary schools in 1932 was just one of the dramatic changes that the government would bring upon education and upon the lives of Iran's women during the next four decades.

The Iranian Ministry of Education also instituted examinations for all students completing the sixth, ninth and eleventh grades. The mission schools were compelled to send their students for these exams, and generally their students excelled. This success caused an influx of new students transferring to Iran Bethel from other schools. In addition, the Ministry of Education so highly appreciated the cooperative attitude of the mission schools during this reorganization that many principals, teachers and other representatives of the American schools were asked to serve on the examining boards.

One example of Iran Bethel's cooperation concerned the girls' uniforms. The Minister of Education advocated uniforms and the girls in most schools wore the prescribed grey ones. However, the girls at Iran Bethel had decided they wanted to design uniforms of their own and had chosen a soft Alice-blue for their jacket and skirt.

One day an inspector came to the school to visit Jane. Looking out the office window at the blue-uniformed girls in the garden, he asked, "Miss Doolittle, what are those costumes I see out there?"

"The uniforms which the girls have designed to wear to school," replied Jane forthrightly.

"Well," he said perfunctorily, "you've got to use the grey ones like everyone else."

So they did.

In January of 1935, Jane was informed of another new decree by the shah: foreign names for schools could no longer be used. Therefore, Iran Bethel was renamed "Nurbakhsh", meaning "light-giving." The school carried on its usual program, however-er.

One of the shah's most controversial programs had to do with Muslim women. He wanted this half of the population to come out from behind their traditional veil, the "chador", and into the mainstream of life. He knew that this decision would have great social, psychological, religious, political and economic implications. So he began by asking his Queen, Taj-ol-Muluk, and her daughters, Princess Shams and Princess Ashraf, to be the first to appear in public without a veil.[2] He also knew that such changes would be best received in the ten to twelve schools where young women were being educated—education, itself, was a change from centuries of tradition. The shah decided that the Ministry of Education's formal presentation of diplomas in January would be an appropriate time for his family's first public appearances without the traditional veil.

Jane recalls the announcement that all the graduates of the eleventh class-which was as far as the schools went at that time—should come with their principals to the Teacher's Training College to receive their diplomas. The girls were to wear long-sleeved white dresses, white stockings and shoes, but no veils, scarfs or hats, and the principals were to wear dark blue. So, on January 7, 1936, Jane took the previous year's eleventh grade classes and went to the College. She recalls:

> The principals and their girls were in one large room while the boys and their principals were in another room. His Majesty, Reza Shah, went into the room where the boys were and presented their diplomas. The Queen and her two daughters, wearing European clothes and hats, came into the room where the girls were. As the names of the schools were called out, the principals went forward to receive the diplomas from the hand of Her Majesty. It was tremendously exciting!

After they received their diplomas and awards, the girls were ordered to line up in the garden, even though it was bitter cold. They were to salute His Majesty, Reza Shah, as he drove off. How thrilled they all were to see his smile of approval as his car moved slowly past them.

Jane continues the story:

> The next morning, all the principals of the schools were called into the office of the Minister of Education. We were told that now that her Majesty and the two princesses had appeared unveiled, it was inappropriate that any Iranian women should go veiled .... Administrators and teachers were urged to get all the girls out of their veils as quickly as possible.

> At Iran Bethel, the students, excited about the unveiling, began a competition to see which class could soonest remove all their veils. Every day there would be whoops of glee as an-other girl would come to school without her veil.

One of Jane's students, Parveneh, remembers that:

> Millons of people had come to see the queen and princesses
> without their chadors. This made everyone feel that it was
> okay. Soon there were official mixed parties, and the universi-
> ties opened to women for the first time . . . . The young women
> had no problem shedding their veils . . . because they wanted
> to be European. However, the older women had trouble with
> the new way for three reasons: first, they were not used to it;
> second, they had a strong belief in the teachings of Islam; and
> third, they didn't know how to dress for public appearance.

In addition to the schools, the shah had other strategies also.
After a certain date, doroshgeh drivers were forbidden to transport women wearing veils. Next came an announcement that entrance to the covered bazaar was forbidden to women who wore
veils—the implications being that this was to reduce shoplifting.
Many older women chose not to go shopping rather than give up
their veils; but as the days stretched into weeks, some of them
weakened in order to return to shopping.

Usually on the shah's birthday there had been two formal re-
ceptions: one for the men and one for the women. However, that
spring Tehran society was set agog by invitations from the shah
and queen for a single reception at the Golestan Palace. Appearing on the handsome invitations, where the initials R.S.V.P. were
usually placed, were the cryptic words, "No excuses will be accepted." The shah knew that some of the older women might try
to excuse themselves by having their husbands say that the
wives were absent because of illness or a sudden emergency.

Another tactic against the centuries-old tradition came with a
newspaper announcement that, from a certain date onward, all
registered prostitutes must wear the chador. Of course, no decent
woman then wanted to be mistaken for a prostitute!

A news article in *Ettelaat* on February 10, 1936, reported that:

> Word from various provinces that (Muslim) religious leaders
> are adopting European costumes and that they and their wives
> are sharing in the celebrations connected with the women's
> movement, shows that there exist a great many of the real re-
> ligious leaders who thoroughly understand the laws of Islam
> and the principles of that true religion, as follows: first, that
> their spirituality and high rank have nothing to do with the

type or shape of their clothing, and that theology is a much higher and greater thing than outward appearance; secondly, that the veil has been the means of concealing the rights and trampling on the social advantages of women, and was only an ill-matched patch of another color upon religion, that the veil has brought many evils to womankind, for whom the true Islamic law has maintained every kind of advantage, and that the same veil has been the cause of plain transgressions from the straight path of religion.

In the midst of the many outward changes, Jane never lost sight of the importance of shaping the students' hearts as well as their behavior, but it wasn't easy to measure what impact the school had on the girls' hearts. One day, as Jane sat in her office reviewing reports, Batul came in with a copy of a Tehran newspaper.[3] She tossed it onto Jane's desk with a mischievous smile. "Excuse me, Miss Doolittle," she said, realizing she was interrupting Jane's work, "there's something I think you ought to read." She smiled again. "There's an article in the newspaper that tells people exactly what you are up to. Keep it if you wish." Then Batul hurried out.

With great interest, Jane laid aside her report and searched the news columns until she found the following item:

If you ever pass through Kamal-ol-molk, for God's sake pay a visit to a ruined old stable in which a family of human beings live. One day I paid a visit to this family. On my entrance to the stable I had to lift up a very dirty canvas curtain full of patches, used as a door. On looking inside I saw a sick old woman lying on a dirty bed and shivering from cold, for it was winter. In another corner I saw an old man who was also sick and lying in bed. His business had been gathering and selling rags and dried pomegranate skins.

At this time a little girl, eight or nine years old, entered the stable. She was very weak and thin. Nevertheless she carried a baby on her shoulders. Her feet were bare and her clothes all in rags. I don't know where she had found the few pieces of stale bread and bit of cooked beet which she had brought for feeding her parents. She was very surprised to see a stranger there.

I don't know if Victor Hugo had seen such a scene. What a chapter he could add to his book, "Les Miserables" .... I tried to stroke her [the child's] head gently and offered her a few sil-

ver coins to make her forget the pain in her head. She did not
accept the money but said, "Sir, we are not beggars." She
showed me the piles of rags and the dried skins of the pome-
granates. "My father has been sick a long time and that is why
our condition is so bad."

I was meditating over this when the curtain was lifted and a
well-dressed young woman about twenty years old entered the
stable. First, I thought she was an angel. Very soon I discovered
that I was mistaken and that the lady was an Iranian. She spoke
with great sympathy to them, asked their condition, and
helped a great deal. Then she turned to me and said, "Doctor,
this old woman has accepted me as her daughter that I may
come here every day and help them as much as possible. Please
tell this little girl of theirs to be quiet, and promise her that her
mother will be all right very soon."

So I tried to quiet the little girl. Also I tried to ask the name of
the kind young woman who had come to help this family and
who had brought some medicine and food for them. She would
not tell me and said, "Doctor, my name would not help you,
and it does not matter if you don't know my name. I can only
tell you that I try to help others as much as I can, and also that I
am a student of the American Girls' School, where I learned
this." In return I said, "Be whoever you want to be. May God
keep you from evil and increase the number of those like you."

Jane sat staring at the the lines; then she took a deep breath as
joy swelled within her. "This is why I came!" she thought. "A
girl from our school, going alone to a wretched old stable right in
her own city, to help her own poverty-stricken countrymen.
Thank you, God, for the beautiful gift this girl is making; may
others of them follow her lead."

NOTES

1. At that time, the Presbyterian Foreign Mission Board generally
gave a first furlough to their missionaries after five years of service. Subsequent furloughs were granted after seven years, though in regions
with severe climates, shorter and more frequent furloughs were arranged.

2. Princess Ashraf recalls the afternoon her father, a Muslim, came to
them saying, "This is the hardest thing I've ever had to do, but I must
ask you to serve as an example for other Persian women." Taken from

Faces In a Mirror, by Ashraf Pahlavi, Prentice-Hall, Inc., Englewood Cliffs, N.J., 1980, p. 25.
   3. Taken from an article appearing in "Ettelaat," dated February 22, 1933.

CHAPTER SEVEN

Is This Where We Die?

In December, 1936, Jane received a message from the New York office of the Presbyterian Board. The Board wrote that Sage Junior College, which was developing in connection with the Nurbakhsh High School, would be separated and developed into a full four-year college for women. Therefore, Jane should go to Beirut to observe the new Beirut College for Women. Under the supervision of Miss Winifred Shannon, Beirut College had established a very fine reputation and its degree bestowed full B.A. status. The plan was that after Jane's visit to the campus in Beirut, she and Miss Shannon would return to Tehran in order to assess the Sage program and give their recommendations to the Board.

"December!" thought Jane, shuddering. "Those people in New York City, with their warm, flatland offices, just don't understand the winter and terrain of Iran." Nevertheless, in early January (1937), Jane packed for the journey. Since Gertrude's mother, Esther Norollah, was beginning a journey to London, the two women traveled the more than 1,000 miles to Beirut together. Much of the way there was barely more than a car-width cleared through the high, cold, white snow piled on both sides of the slippery road. Jane and Esther frequently exchanged prayerful glances.

However, their skillful driver was able to deliver them safely to Baghdad, from where they took the desert bus to Beirut.

After assisting Mrs. Norollah to make her shipboard connections for London, Jane went on to the American College for Women. She was warmly welcomed by Miss Shannon and spent the next several days visiting the college classes, interviewing the teachers and evaluating the program. She found many similarities between the two schools. However, Beirut College was a separate institution, whereas in Tehran the educational program continued from grammar school through high school and on to college.

As scheduled, Jane and Miss Shannon left Beirut for Tehran. They arrived in Kermanshah two days later where they stopped at a miserable hotel. They contacted the mission to inquire about travel conditions ahead. Actual information was hard to come by, though opinions were everywhere. Uncertain as to what to do, Jane and Winifred specifically asked God for His leading.

At their 5:00 A.M. breakfast the next morning, they were pleased to have the Rev. Dr. Cady Allen join them. Dr. Allen had just reached Kermanshah the day before from Hamadan and had traveled through heavy snow. In fact, it had taken him five days to cover the 120 miles usually completed in one short day's run. He was anxious to set them on their way immediately. "The road is clear right now," he advised, "and you ought to hurry as fast as possible before another storm hits." So, with another traveler, an Englishman, joining them in their car, Jane and Winifred proceeded on, carrying Dr. Allen's messages to those in Hamadan.

On reaching the foot of the famous Abassabad Pass in the Zagros Mountains, the party stopped at a teahouse to ask for the latest information. However, only the Englishman and the driver could enter, since teahouses were solely for men. The driver reported back to Jane and Winifred that nothing had come through all morning and no one should proceed until someone made it through from the other end. The women were already practically frozen to their seats, and on hearing this they looked at each other totally speechless. There was nothing they could do so they continued to sit in their car. They sat there all that night, all the next day and all the next night!

By Sunday morning, five other cars were pulled up behind them. In these cars were an Iranian officer who was returning to Tehran with five young Iranians who'd just completed their courses in naval tactics in Italy. The officer was adamant that their cars must go on, and the women decided that if he thought he could get through, so could their car.

So, the six-car caravan began the long, slow trip over the pass.

In front of the cars, heavily bundled villagers struggled laboriously to dig out the snow-buried road. Inch-by-inch the cars crawled up the mountain. The cars progressed so slowly that sometimes Jane and Winifred took turns walking. They would walk until tired, then get back into the car to join their traveling companion. The Englishman patiently sat the day out, quietly enduring in disciplined silence.

At about 5:00 P.M. the cars finally reached the guard post near the summit of the 12,000-foot high pass. The guardhouse was a small two-room mud shelter built for a single guard. Here, all the Iranian men in the cars got out, shaking themselves, and hurried off in the direction of the guardhouse. After several attempts, the Englishman managed to get himself uncramped and dislodged from his seat. Stiffly, he limped up the pathway after the other men, leaving Jane and Winifred behind. It never occurred to either of the women to try to follow the men into the guardhouse; such a thing just was not done.

A storm closed in and the guardhouse was lost to view. There was total silence inside the car except for the sounds of water dripping from the boiling hot engine and spluttering loudly on the icy road beneath. Soon even this sound ceased. The two shivering women began to assess their situation. Here they were, again,marooned outside in the freezing cold with only the clothes on their backs. Their baggage was strapped onto the car and was unavailable. A bag of food was at hand—but it was necessary to remove the bulky warmth of the gloves to get into it.

"Well," announced Jane, "we've still got a few crackers left. And, I feel a crooked and bent banana—one, two, another!" The crackers and the bananas had been intended to be gifts, for they were hard to find in Iran and therefore a special treat. "And here," continued Jane, "how's this for absolute luxury—a tin of sardines!" The women laughed at the ridiculous fare they had to share.

"The life of a missionary—really unreal sometimes, isn't it?" observed Winifred.

"Few people know!" acknowledged Jane.

They remembered that the Bible contained numerous accounts of important mountaintop experiences. Praying together, they asked the Lord God Almighty to protect them while on this mountaintop. After presenting themselves into His loving care, they fell asleep, exhausted by the rigorous day of travel.

They were hungry when they awoke, and struggled to get the sardine can open, being very careful not to spill any oil. But when they saw the frozen sardines, they chuckled at their foolish precautions. Periodically, they quenched their thirst by grabbing handfuls of snow from the top of the car.

Now and then, the driver would make his way to the car to see if they were still surviving. Jane would ask, "Isn't there something hot to drink that we could have? Don't you have a stove where we could get warm?" But the driver would reply, "No, nothing" and then trudge back through the drifts to the guardhouse.

By now the storm was worse, their food was gone, and Jane and Winifred could see and hear wolves in the distance. "We cannot endure another night in this car!" Jane declared. They opened the door and crawled out, barely able to stand. Forcing themselves to move, they looked everywhere for a sign or sound of life but could see no path or footstep to follow.

"Let's start in the direction the other's went," suggested Jane, crunching inch-by-inch forward through the deep, fresh drifts. Awkwardly they stumbled on until, what was that, the guardhouse? Yes! They pushed with all their might at the door and it opened! The women stepped inside. Panting and weak, they stared. There were the men, comfortable and warm, sitting around a nice hot stove. The men's talking and laughing died out at once. Then poor Winifred, wobbling and weaving, fainted. At this, some of the men moved to make a place for her.

Jane loosened Winifred's heavy outer garments, and then her own. Gently, she worked to get Winifred's circulation in motion, and soon the exhausted woman came to. After endless hours of freezing cold, the shock of the heat had been too much for her to bear. One of the men gave them an orange. Jane peeled it and gave Winifred the first section—it tasted like heavenly manna. Then someone else got them hot tea and their frozen bodies began to revive.

The guardhouse, indeed, had very little space. However, there was a small old shed attached where the trunks of two big trees, split down the middle, were stored. The men got together and, by kicking and yanking, pushed the two slabs side-by-side. Then, the women lay their "pustines" (fur coats) over the wood, and thankfully laid themselves down to sleep. How good it felt to be able to stretch out.

Early the next morning, the men came through this shed "bedroom" to look out the door. "Bah!" they muttered in angry disgust; a new storm had obliterated all signs of the shoveling they'd done for the last two days. With the scarce food getting scarcer, two of the navy men decided to leave and find a village to get some help. Jane and Winifred, along with some others, decided that if the two men could find their way out, they could too. So out they went.

The group walked and walked—not on the road, wherever that was—down the side of the mountain, and finally reached a village. The navy students took the two women into a house where they all could stay. Inside was the most wonderful object in the world to their cold limbs, a coorsie. The women sat on the floor on mattresses with the others, and everyone warmed themselves under the quilts. The entire party stayed at the house for the next couple of days. The kind villagers brought them hot soup, bread and hot tea. By now, Jane and Winifred had almost lost track of time.

They were dumbfounded when a villager from the other side of the pass arrived with a telegram for Jane. "It's from Gertrude," said Jane in astonishment. "She's wondering where we are and what's happening? It's a wonder we ever received this at all!" Jane gave the villager her reply—"We're all right."—and some coins in gratitude for the unbelievable effort he'd made to bring a message of concern.

Jane kept wondering how she and Winifred were ever going to get to Tehran. There was still no possibility of cars getting through, and Hamadan, she surmised, was probably still ten to twenty miles away. The two women decided to start walking again, and so did many of the others.

About this time, an Iranian major, traveling with his wife and child, showed up and took charge. The major led the way as they tramped along, feet up and down, up and down, up and down. Jane had on rubber galoshes, but Winifred had brought nothing at all for such snowy walking. Her badly shrunken shoes made each step very painful. The women found a pair of heavy woolen socks which Jane helped Winifred pull on. At one point, the major gave his coat to his child; and at another, he commandeered a horse for himself and his family.

After a while, Jane and Winifred got ahead of the major's party and into another village. There, Jane hired one of the village boys to go ahead into Hamadan with a message to the mission explaining that they were trying to get there. In the meantime, the women continued walking. After some miles, they reached a teahouse, and this time, regardless of custom, they went in to rest and dry out their socks.

Suddenly, the boy they'd sent to Hamadan reappeared. On his way he had met a missionary from Hamadan. He now gave Jane a note. She read: "We have come out to find you, but it's getting so late and dark we are afraid we won't be able to get back into town so we are returning to Hamadan. We will try again tomorrow." The women were past tears. They were so near, yet it felt like a million footsteps away. Jane thanked the messenger and gave him a few more rials for his welcome assistance. Then the two sank into heavy silence.

As they sat together in the tea house, they were startled to hear what sounded like horses' hooves coming toward them. A carriage rolled straight in their direction and stopped right outside! Jane got to her feet and faced the door. Two men, a driver and a young Persian lad, came hurrying inside and spotted the two women instantly. "Khanum Doolittle?"

Jane couldn't believe her ears! She moved towards him to receive the note he offered.

> Dear Jane:
> On our way back we found this carriage which had just taken some people to another village. We've engaged the driver to come for you and have sent one of our Persian students along with the driver to be sure that you are the ones they bring back. We'll see you soon. God keep you safe.
> H.M.

Jane and the student, Mohebi, began animated Persian conversation, not a word of which Winifred understood. Mohebi helped the women into the carriage and they started, lighthearted as well as light-headed, down the treacherous road. Mohebi explained to Jane that as the carriage was on its way to pick them up, they'd passed the major who stopped them and tried to bargain, negotiate and otherwise commandeer the carriage for himself. But Mohebi had insisted, showing Hugo Muller's note, and the major let the carriage go on.

The missionaries had sent some sandwiches along and the food tasted delicious. However, Mohebi cautioned them not to eat everything now, in case they weren't able to reach Hamadan that night.

In describing these events years later, Commodore Fischer said:

> Mr. Payne, the mission treasurer, received a telegram from Kermanshah asking if the two women had arrived? No! came the reply. He then sent the telegram on to our mission in Hamadan. We hadn't known that Jane was enroute, so she must be up there somewhere, snowbound! No mail or other messages were coming through.
>
> Hugo Muller came to the school to tell me more about the situation and to say that he would postpone his classes to go out and help. A student, Mohebi, overheard the conversation and promptly said, "I must go too. I would give my life for them!"
>
> They drove their car as far as they could, parked at the foot of the mountain, and started trudging up through the deeply-packed snow. In time they met some men coming down who said that two American women, also on foot, were trying to make it out too. Hugo and Mohebi pushed on faster but darkness finally overtook them. They decided to turn back, planning to try again the next day. But they located a carriage, and Mohebi went back with carriage and driver to find the women.
>
> When Mohebi finally reached them, Winifred's feet were so swollen she could hardly walk. Her shoes had long ago shrunk and she was trying to get down through the snow in her bare stocking feet. Mohebi gave her his heavy shoes and came back down in his thick woolen socks.

As Jane and Winifred rode along in the carriage, they agreed that, under the circumstances, this was preferable to walking and driving. Villagers continued to work to clear the road for cars, but how long it would be before cars and baggage would connect with them, they did not know. Nodding and weary, the women were still bravely enduring.

It was about 10:00 P.M., and very dark, when the carriage drew up in front of the huge, double gates of the Hamadan compound; a flood of memories swooped down on Jane. The Hugo Mullers and other friends took them in, providing a welcome that Jane and Winifred would never forget. Here, within the loving warmth of this God-given haven, the women rested for a couple of days.

Yet, Jane and Winifred still needed to reach Tehran, so after the rest, they started anew. Two or three of the cars had made it down from the mountaintop and the women were fortunate in locating the car carrying their baggage. Fervently praying they would reach Tehran that night, they continued the journey once more by car. Thankfully they watched the miles go by. But in the last glimmer of daylight they suddenly saw snow drifts looming up before them in the road. The wind, taking advantage of the broad plain below, was blowing at its worst.

Keenly disappointed, but accepting the situation, they located the only caravanserie for miles around. However, when they arrived they learned that a European couple had taken the last room in the place. Jane and Winifred looked into this room, hoping the couple would give them some space; but no, these Europeans were not used to sharing a bedroom. Moving down the hall, they looked through another open door and discovered their earlier companions, the naval students. The women were immediately invited in, and they all gathered around the stove to wait out another long night. The coal-burning stove, however, gave off toxic fumes, and by morning both Jane and Winifred had splitting headaches.

By early daylight the wind died down and the villagers continued hacking and shoveling the mounds of snow off the road. The drivers lit fires under the engines to get the motors running; then the travelers piled inside the autos and the entourage started off again.

Gertrude, and all of Iran Bethel, rejoiced when Jane and Winifred finally arrived. They had been anxious and had said many prayers for their safety. Previously, Jane had made the journey from Beirut to Damascus to Kermanshah to Hamadan to Tehran in about three days. But, caught in one of the worst snowstorms recorded in Iranian history, this trip had taken two weeks!

Soon, however, the two women were underway with their assigned responsibilities. Winifred went about inspecting the school, visiting classes and interviewing teachers. The outcome was that she and Jane agreed that the work of the Sage College students was equivalent to that of the Beirut Women's College, and that Nurbakhsh should be separated from Sage college. This would allow the latter to develop independently.

Subsequently, Winifred Shannon was appointed by the New York Presbyterian Board to return to Tehran and develop the new college. She became chief administrator in August, 1937. The old Mir Shaker building, originally the small dormitory opened by Charlotte Young for Iran Bethel, now accommodated Sage College. The first year, 100 students enrolled, and many of these Sage College graduates went on to important positions within the country.

Map of Iran showing principal mission stations of the Board of Foreign Missions
of the Presbyterian Church of the U.S.A., 1934-1934.

Orrin Sage Doolittle, Jane's
father.

Grace Ferguson Doolittle,
Jane's mother.

The big roomy Doolittle home (dark siding) in Yonkers. Jane's second floor room shows parted white curtains.

The gentleman gardener—Jane's father enjoying a favorite hobby at his home.

Wells College (Founded 1868) main building. The 360 acre campus on the eastern shore of Cayuga Lake (one of the Fingerlakes) is in the village of Aurora, New York, 25 miles north of Cornell University, and about an hour's drive to the cities of Syracuse and Rochester. Seven colleges and universities are within a half hour of Wells, one of the nation's first women's colleges.

(Above) 19221—Jane Doo-
little (2nd from left) and
friends at intermission of
the YWCA cabinet meet-
ing, Wells College.

(Right) 1921—Jane (left)
and her Cornell friend, Lois
Osborn, sitting on the
bumper of Lois's car at
Wells College.

"The Evangelization of the World in this Generation"

THE BULLETIN

Published by the New York State Student Volunteer Union

| VOL. V. | NOVEMBER, 1920 | No 2. |

Announcing

Eighteenth Annual Conference
New York State Student Volunteer Union

Wells College

Aurora, New York

December Third, Fourth and Fifth

Nineteen Hundred and Twenty

The Student Volunteer Conference

DURING the week-end of December 4th, 5th, and 6th the annual conference of the New York State Student Volunteer Movement was held at Wells College. This conference was one of the most broadening influences which came to the college during the year. The colleges and universities were, Cornell, Buffalo, Elmira, New York State College for Teachers, Vassar, Union, Hartwick, Skidmore, Syracuse, Houghton, Rochester, Genesee, Wesleyan, William Smith, Potsdam, Hobart, Colgate, Clarkson Tech., and Auburn Theological Seminary. That the conference was so great a success, was due to the very able management of the Wells' chairmen and the interested co-operation of the entire student body. The chairmen of the various committees were as follows:

General Manager	JANE DOOLITTLE
Local Arrangements	CORILLA BRODNAX
Reception	MARY LLOYD
Registration	MARGARET TRIMBLE
Waiting on Tables	ELIZABETH VAN DORN
Information	GERTRUDE ELFORD
Lost and Found	ELEANOR DEVLIN
Literature	GRACE MOLDENHAWER
Music	MISS ELLIS

The first meeting of the conference was held in the college chapel, Friday evening. President Macmillan spoke a few words of welcome. Mr. James S. Lewis of the Methodist Board gave an address on "Seeing the World," illustrated by lantern slides. Mr. Frank Eckerson of the Reformed Board gave the following address on the "World Call." Everyone felt, at the end of the evening, that the spirit of the conference had been expressed.

108

Significant leadership activities for Jane Doolittle were related to the Student Volunteer programs.

Jane Elizabeth Doolittle
1921 graduate of Wells College.

This Wells College coach is used each year for graduating Senior ceremonies.

May, 1924, Tehran. Charlotte Young and Jane enjoyed a deep and very special friendship.

Taq-i-Bustan. A few miles east of Karamanshah (founded A.D. 390) are the famous rock carvings in the caves of Taq-i-Bustan. A vast pool at the foot of the mountain collects the waters of a small stream. Between the pool and the rock face is a garden where fragments of the Sassanid period are found. Carvings on the rock face depict the investiture of Ardeshir II (379-383).

In the second cave on the two side walls are found carvings of royal hunts. The king, standing erect with bow and arrow, is shooting wild boar. He is being rowed across a swamp escorted by boatfuls of female musicians entertaining him.

(Above) The Cyrus Cylinder, a ten-inch-long clay barrel (discovered 1879 in Mesopotamia, now housed in the British Museum in London) shows the Sumerian inscription written in cuneiform telling how Cyrus the Great (559-529 B.C.) conquered the king of Babylon. "I am Cyrus, the king of the world, great king." It gives an account of his benevolent acts, among them a decree permitting exiled Jews to return to Jerusalem (538 B.C.). Though the cylinder does not specifically refer to this decree, it does note Cyrus's general policy of returning exiles and their possessions to their homelands: "I (also) gathered all their (former) inhabitants and returned (to them) their habitations."

(Below) Thought to be the Tomb of Esther, queen of Xerxes (King Ahasuerus, 5th Century B.C.) in Hamadan. (Copyright 1988 by M. Ali Issari.)

SHOPKEEPER

STUDIO Hayrapeṭiʼu

HUBBLE-BUBBLE: a tobacco pipe so arranged tha the smoke passes through water making a bubbling sound. Like *HOOKAH:* a pipe with a long flexible stem so arranged that the smoke is cooled by passing through water. Also similar to *NARGHILE* of Indian origin, an oriental apparatus for smoking tobacco.

Winter, 1936 at Tehran Teacher's College: Reza Shah comes to inspect the results of his historic decree that women must henceforth abandon use of the chardor, the traditional veil.

(Left) Jane Elizabeth Doolittle, principal/head-mistress of Iran Bethel.

(Below) 1966, Tehran. The Minister of Education honors Jane Doolittle with a special award for her 50 years of outstanding service to the girls and women of Iran.

Jane Doolittle expresses appreciation for the love she had received through the years.

(Below) PERSEPOLIS: It was here in October 1971 that Iran celebrated 2500 years of monarchial rule. Guests invited to attend the 4 day commemoration included many of the world's heads of state and celebrities from many walks of life. PERSEPOLIS is ancient Persia's greatest city and is located in southwestern Iran. Darius (became king in 521 B.C.) started this building project about 500 B.C. for ceremonial celebrations related to their No Ruz festival (beginning March 21 and continuing for 13 days). Later kings Xerxes and Artaxerxes carried on the building plans.

1975, Tehran. Elizabeth Kay Voorhees meets Jane Doolittle
and Gertrude Norollah in the garden of their residence.

1979. At the Doolittle clinic in Tehran Jane greets new patients.

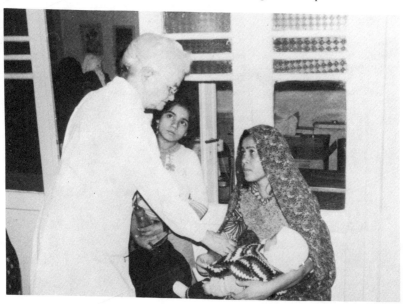

1979. At the Doolittle Clinic entrance Jane comforts a waiting patient.

At the Clinic Jane registers the patients awaiting attention and care.

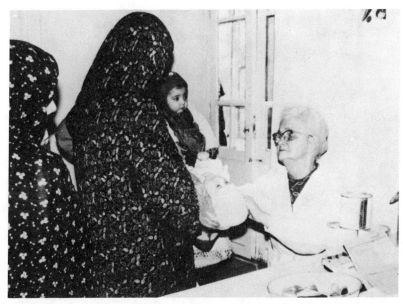

(Above) April 1980: Jane Doolittle, suddenly homeless, sitting alone in a motel room in Meridian, CT., (a town where her uncle had once served as a mayor and had been a banker) wonders what is next? "Thy Word is a lamp unto my feet . . ." Whither?

(Below) 1980. Jane in her new home-away-from-home, rejoices in God's Word and His loving care of her needs.

1980. Long-time friend of college days, Lois Osborn, motivates people in her town to find and furnish a residence for the now-homeless Jane and her Iranian friend, Gertrude Norollah.

At their Cortland residence, Jane Doolittle and Gertrude Norollah challenge each other in their nightly Scrabble contest.

(Above) April, 1981. Duarte, California. The late Dr. William Wysham greets his long-time associates, Gertrude Norollah and Jane Doolittle, at his Westminster Gardens home.

1988, at her residence in Cortland, New York, Jane continues to serve God in every way possible.

CHAPTER EIGHT

Crying for Love

In 1938, Jane was once again pulling into New York Harbor, looking forward to a year of renewal and refreshment with her family. She quickly blended into a familiar routine: becoming reacquainted with her loved ones, accepting invitations to speak before groups supportive of the work in Iran; re-enrolling at Columbia University for further graduate study; and catching up on all that had been happening in her native land. Under the new president, Franklin Roosevelt, the country was struggling through deep economic depression and was gravely concerned about the political events in Europe which threatened to engulf the world in war. Jane wondered what effect these circumstances would have on Iran.

All too soon, it seemed, her furlough ended and Jane said good-bye to her family. However, she was pleased to be returning to Iran with a new Sage College teacher, Sylvia Sherk, the daughter of former missionaries to Iran. Through Sylvia, an important new dimension would be added to the school's curriculum and outreach.

As the two women traveled along, a question lurked in Jane's mind. The last time she returned from furlough, she had barely arrived in the country when she was given news about the transfer of all primary school education to the Iranian government. Would another surprise await her this time? When she reached Baghdad, a message was indeed waiting for her: "Hurry on to Iran immediately. Send back the teacher you've just hired for Sage College."

Jane was shocked! What was going on? She left Sylvia in Baghdad and hurried on to Kermanshah where she learned what had happened—all schools directed by foreigners were to be taken over immediately by the Ministry of Education. With the shah's increasing concern for his country, he no longer wanted foreign influence over the young and susceptible.

Jane's mother, upon hearing this news and thinking that Jane would soon return home, sent a one-word cable: "Hallelujah!" But Jane did not see it that way. She had been sent to Iran to share Christ. With her knowledge of the language and her love for the people, surely God would find new channels of service for her. She decided she would await His leading, even though many of her colleagues would leave the country. It was a hard decision and, in the days ahead, the refrain —"I need Thee, Oh, I need Thee, Every hour I need Thee"—often came to mind.

As before, the Mission Board responded cooperatively to the new governmental regulation. Upon advice from Washington D.C., the Board sent a commission to Iran to settle matters with the Ministry of Education. The representatives expected to stay a month or two. However, negotiations went on for most of the school year and during this time all the mission schools continued as usual. As soon as it became evident that the negotiations would take more time, Sylvia Sherk was ordered to proceed to Tehran from Baghdad. When Jane had arrived in Tehran, she found the school maintaining its schedule and she once again took over administration of Nurbakhsh while Winifred Shannon carried on at Sage College. By speeding up the classes, four girls were graduated from Sage College, having completed a four-year course in three years.

Many of the students, disappointed and bewildered by the new ruling, observed Jane with particular interest. As always, her attitude toward them was friendly and concerned. Though she was a strict disciplinarian, the girls knew Jane loved them and wanted only the best for them, and they drew from her quiet strength and example.

When the negotiations were completed, Sage College was closed and some of its students registered at the University of Tehran. Most of the Nurbakhsh students continued their studies on the same property, but under Ministry of Education control, using what had been the Sage College dormitory as their school building.

With the transfer of responsibility to the Ministry of Education, Jane was faced with the need to find a new place to live. She wanted to find accommodations which would not only provide easy access to food, supplies and transportation, but would also make it possible for her to continue to teach. After a long and thorough search, Jane was relieved and pleased to find a new building containing a ground-floor apartment with good-sized rooms. It was handily situated in the center of Lalezar, the big mid-city shopping district. Jane invited Gertrude Norollah and Golebehar, the cook, to share the apartment with her. The three worked together to create a pleasant, harmonius environment in their new quarters.

They weren't in the apartment very long, however, before they became aware that the leaves on all of Gertrude's plants were shrivelling up and dying. There was also a very peculiar odor pervading the place, day and night. They began investigating to find out why. The apartment's outside entrance door led to a teahouse which had a basement with windows. Peering into these windows one day, Jane and Gertrude saw men lying all around the floor smoking on pipes. It was an opium den! This accounted for the peculiar odor. They were literally face-to-face with one of Iran's great problems, drug addiction.

Despite this unexpected drawback, the apartment was a nice one. It provided adequate living space for the three women and room where Jane could teach those students wanting to continue their education. Three of Jane's students were trying to finish their B.A. degrees, and others came to her to improve their English and general knowledge. Jane's teaching was possible, in part, because the American churches who had been supporting her decided to continue sending their gifts as long as Jane felt that God wanted her in Iran.

One of the students tells what this time of study with Jane meant to her:

> Some of us worked with Miss Doolittle in small classes at her home. Each day we were greeted at the door by Golebehar, a very kind soul. As each of us completed the requirements for our degree, we would receive our diploma, but sometimes without a graduation ceremony. I was entitled to my diploma but every time I would ask Miss Doolittle when I would get it

she would matter-of-factly say, "It is not ready yet as it has to be signed by Dr. Jordan" [of Alborz College which shared accreditation from the state of New York with Sage College]. This kept going on for a couple of months.

Little did I know that she was waiting to make the great presentation of my diploma on my wedding day! Of all the beautiful gifts I received, that diploma was one of the most treasured! I can still see that picture in front of me: Miss Doolittle walking towards me through the door of the grand ballroom of the hotel with my diploma clasped in her hands. What a thrill.

And I remember the commencement when Miss Doolittle was being honored and the Minister of Education spoke up and said, "Her name should have been Do Much instead of Do Little!"

One morning after an early shopping errand, Golebehar returned to the apartment to find a little boy sitting on the doorstep, crying mournfully. The little boy would, unknowingly, bring a whole new ministry to which Jane would selflessly and energetically devote the next three decades of her life in Iran.

Being mindful of Jane's interests and motivation, Golebehar questioned him and then came hurrying in to find Jane. "Khanum," she said in Persian, "there's a little boy outside on our doorstep. He's weeping and sad because he can't go to school. He doesn't have the uniforms, books, paper and pencil that he needs. Won't you go do something about it?"

Jane asked the little boy where he lived. He took her to an old caravanserai, a big open courtyard surrounded by mud buildings. Once the many small rooms had been used as resting places for the camel drivers after they had unloaded their animals in the courtyard. Now, it was the permanent dwelling for about forty families, and each windowless room was occupied by four to ten people. The residents shared one outside toilet and one big open pool filled with jube water for washing.

The little boy, Haji, proudly took the American lady to meet his astonished family. "Who was this strange foreigner who spoke their own language so fluently? Why was she with their little Haji?" they wondered. Haji's mother was stone deaf and her six children used sign language to communicate with her. She often did other people's laundry and housework to help support the family. Her husband, a tall sickly-looking man, was a "tabaghkesh," a man who carried large round wooden trays loaded with goods on his head. (Because of the terrific weights they carried, many of these porters eventually went blind.)

None of Haji's brothers and sisters went to school. One of the brothers, perhaps ten years old, worked as a butcher's assistant. One morning just after the shop opened an Army officer came to buy meat. The man asked for his meat "without bone" but paid the boy the much cheaper rate for "with bone." When the boy objected, the man hit him. Having the butcher's knife in his hand, the brother struck back, killing the man. As a result, the boy had been sent to prison.

As Jane became acquainted with the families in that caravanserai, they took her to meet other friends in other caravanserais who, in turn, took her to meet their friends. In this way, Jane became aware of some of Iran's poorest and neediest people.

Haji's eldest sister came to live in Jane's household for a couple years, and Jane started having Friday meetings for the children of the caravanserai which she called the Friday School. Friday School was patterned after the American Sunday School, with stories, handwork, singing and games. Then Jane decided that if the children were to be truly helped, their mothers must also receive some training. So, Jane began holding Wednesday meetings in her home for the mothers. The mothers would sit on the living room floor in the customary style while Golebehar served them tea and cookies. Then Jane would teach them how to sew, knit and spin, as well as easily learned songs. It was a treat to have somebody care about them, and the mothers loved to sing. Before they left, Jane would tell them Bible stories about her loving God.

Jane soon realized that many of the mothers had serious health problems. The very ill she sent to the mission hospital. When it was closed by the U.S. Army during World War II she sent them to the Iranian government facilities. But the women didn't receive the medicine they needed, nor did they seem to improve. So, at Jane's urging, a doctor friend agreed to see the women in his office, which he did until it became too big a responsibility. Then Jane searched for another solution. One of the Sage College graduates had completed her medical training at the University of Tehran and she consented to give a couple of hours a week to help these women. Thus, Jane opened a Wednesday afternoon clinic. The clinic had one doctor, one nurse and one staff person—Jane—to take care of all the details.

At first the Wednesday afternoon clinic had only two or three patients on a regular basis. Soon there were sixteen and then more than sixty. Another doctor and nurse came to help and gradually the clinic began to acquire and distribute the prescriptive medicines which the patients needed. Eventually, the heightened interest of the Iran Bethel graduates in what Jane was doing to help their own people would lead to the establishment of the "Doolittle Clinic."

Gertrude, likewise, embarked on a new career about this time. Her former school was closed, so Gertrude began "Noor School," a girl's finishing school which offered classes in English, sewing and cooking. Later, Gertrude taught the students to make character dolls and animals. These were sold for charity and became very popular with the large foreign community.

During these days, most Iranians were fearful that, once again, Iran, because of its strategic geographical location, was going to be caught up in the growing tensions between Europe and Asia. These fears were realized in September, 1941, when the Allies invaded Iran. Twenty-two days later, Reza Shah abdicated his throne in favor of his twenty-two year old son, Mohammad Reza Pahlavi. The shah desperately hoped that the Pahlavi dynasty would continue its leadership in programs to guide Iran out of the Middle Ages. Thus it was that Mohammad Reza Pahlavi assumed the role of "Shahanshah," King of Kings, of Iran.

The war years were hard for Iran just as they were for many other nations. In an article written after the War, Jane described some of what it was like living in Tehran then.

> In [America] people know little of Iran and no one realizes what their poverty and undernourishment conditions are. I was interested when I conducted an experienced Red Cross worker, who thought she had seen the worst of bad conditions in the world, through one of the poor districts to see some of my friends there. When we came out from the courtyard into the street, the lady began to be actively ill because of the living conditions she had just seen! I had various classes for these

women and their children, as well as relief and medical work. They learned something of how to sew and also a bit about cleanliness, but there is still a tremendous amount to do .... I live with the people, and they come to my house at any hour for whatever their needs, beginning in the summer before 6:00 A.M. and in the winter before 7:00.

Of course, during the war years we had plenty of troops in Iran and I got to know some of them quite well—at least the British and Americans, who, unfortunately had little opportunity to get to know the fine Persian people, and therefore were not very fond of Iran! Every Saturday evening, a group of soldiers ... would come to our house for a few hours, studying the Bible and praying together. Some days they came to tea, and others for a home-cooked meal. This was the only place in Tehran where the British and American soldiers could socialize together. Their salaries were so different and the British were unable to enjoy restaurants the American boys often used.

In her efforts among the poor, Jane recruited many fine people to help. One such person was Vigen, a young Armenian lad whose whole life was changed as a result. As he tells it:

One Sunday morning after church services, a noble lady approached me. I was 14 years of age. She asked, "Do you want to help at our Friday School?" I said, "Yes, I'll be glad to." And that was the beginning of the most wonderful and lasting relationship with someone who, in the course of the years, has come to be like my spiritual mother.

There is so much I can say about Jane Doolittle. I believe no one's life has been more deeply touched by her than mine .... When I finished theological training at the Beirut Seminary and was getting ready to be ordained for the Christian ministry, Miss Doolittle sent me a note inviting me to her office. I went and we had a private conference together. She prayed for me and my work, for the responsibility that I was going to take over. She said how difficult it was to be a minister of the Gospel in a non-Christian country ....

So, at times, naturally, I would face some problem. I would have my low days. I would be disappointed. I would be frustrated, discouraged ... and there she was every time I called her! As a matter of fact, she has been my life counselor. I couldn't have had a better one, ever in my life!

When World War II ended, it was time for Jane to go to America on her furlough. However, traveling between New York and Tehran in postwar 1946 was not easy. Mr. Payne, the mission treasurer, arranged for Jane and two friends, Fatie, an Iranian teacher, and Edith Lamme, another missionary, to go via Bombay to San Francisco. So, with loving wishes and happy farewells from their friends, the three women boarded a small local plane with eighteen other passengers to go to Zahedan near the Indian border (present-day Pakistan).

The craft was manned by Americans and had bucket seats lining the walls. After a three-hour, 600-mile flight to Mashad, it made a brief landing. There, missionary friends came to meet the three and shared refreshments. Then the flight continued on its final leg to Zahedan. They flew for another three hours through a dense orange haze of dust, entirely without radio connections of any sort. After a long while, the pilot came back to inform the passengers, "We cannot find Zahedan. We must turn back to Mashad!" This was a great disappointment, especially for Jane who was suffering from air sickness. Back in Mashad, the missionary friends were recontacted and they returned to pick up the three travelers, offering them hospitality for the night.

Next morning, the hosts got the trio back to the airport for a 7:00 A.M. departure. Heartier farewells were voiced this time as the travelers were bid "au'voir." However, the wrong kind of fuel had been delivered to the airfield and the plane could not take off until the proper fuel was brought out from the city and poured in the tanks. But at last, sometime after 9:00 A.M., the plane once again took off for Zahedan.

Back in their seats, the travelers fervently hoped they'd get to their destination on time; most of them had other travel connections to meet. They strained to catch a glimpse of their surroundings, but once again the plane was totally enveloped in a dense orange haze that created extremely hazardous conditions with no visibility. After some time, the pilot came on to inform his passengers that they would have to again return to Mashad. By way of emphasizing the dilemma, he added that the plane had all but crashed into a mountain which had suddenly risen up in front of them! When they arrived back in Mashad, the missionary friends again graciously provided lodging and hospitality for the frustrated travelers.

The next morning, pilot and passengers were all assembled and ready to go before dawn, hoping to travel before the orange-colored heat haze developed. This time the travelers were wished "God-speed." Jane laughs as she recalls the experience:

We literally followed the road beneath us for all the long miles that finally led us safely to Zahedan. There other missionary friends came to meet us and take us in. The area is quiet as a tomb and our friends said that not once in the preceding days had they ever heard sounds of a plane . . . . Only God knows where we were flying all those many hours we spent up in the air!

As soon as they and their baggage had landed, Jane and her companions went to the home of British missionaries, Dr. and Mrs. Setralker, who maintained a hospital there. Their hosts informed them that the weekly train from Zahedan into India had waited more than twenty-four hours for their plane, but finally had to go on. Therefore, the stranded travelers had to wait out all the intervening days in this spot which Jane describes as "the most God-forsaken desert town I have ever seen in my life." Despite the fact that fresh food came in from India only once a week, they were well-cared for by the good doctor, his wife, a nurse and their two children.

Jane was concerned that this unexpected delay would cause them to miss their ship at Bombay. They could only count the days and hope. At last, the train returned from Bombay. After grateful farewells to their kind hosts, the travelers boarded the train. Chugging over the desolate miles, they finally reached the steamy port of Bombay and were welcomed at a British missionary hostel. There they received the good news that their ship was still not ready to depart; in fact, they waited in Bombay another week before boarding.

On board, they were dismayed to learn that ship company rules required Asians to be separate from Europeans. Fatie, Miss Lamme and Jane were all assigned to different quarters, each occupying a cabin with eight to ten other passengers. However, they settled in, hoping there would be no more problems. These comforting thoughts lasted but a few hours after they'd set sail. The ship began to pitch and roll as it entered a monsoon, and everyone on board, with the exception of Miss Lamme, became sea sick. Poor Jane could not even lift her head from her bunk for several days.

When the worst of this was over, the emergency alarms rang and the passengers were ordered out on deck for life-belt and safety drills. The cause: left-over war mines were still floating around in the ocean! These drills were frequently repeated as the ship plowed its watery way to first Hong Kong, then Manila and, finally, San Francisco.

In San Francisco, Edith Lamme parted company with her friends, while Jane and Fatie continued together. Jane's mother had notified some of Jane's Wells College friends of her forthcoming arrival and the two travelers were hosted at a celebration dinner in a fine restaurant. Jane also had a great stack of mail to work through, as well as to make contact with the Board of Foreign Missions in New York.

After a few days in San Francisco, Jane and Fatie started the 3,000 mile trek cross-country by train. Two days later, Jane and her family had a joyous reunion at the railroad station in Harmon, New York. There to greet her were her father and mother, her sister and brother-in-law, and her brother, Jed. Loading in baggage and travelers, they drove to the family home in Yonkers. Later that afternoon, the Doolittles took Fatie to Columbia University in New York City. Registering for classes and settling in at the International House marked the fulfillment of a lifetime dream for Fatie—being in the U.S. for study.

"How we praise God," Jane's father remarked later when they finally had time to be together, "for your safety during these last difficult years."

And her mother said wistfully, "Oh, Jane, how much I had hoped that you could come home to stay in 1940. I just felt that you'd given enough of your life to Iran, but I guess—"

Her parents' remarks reminded Jane of a conversation she'd had with Samuel Zwemer when they crossed the desert to Iran in 1926. "Do nothing out of selfish ambition," he had suggested. "Serving is an authentic expression of Christ's love." He had then gone on to explain that a Christian servant is one who willingly relinquishes his or her personal rights and wishes in order to follow Christ's example of serving others. Jane realized that her parents had given her a tremendous gift in their understanding and willingness to let her go thousands of miles from home to share her life with others. They had served the Lord in ways she hadn't always appreciated.

Jane enjoyed being home in the big comfortable house filled with fragrant bouquets from her father's garden. Being frequently in pain, she again went to see the specialist about her back, and learned that a third spinal fusion was necessary. Jane hoped it would be the last. She had been planning to stay only a year, but in March of 1947, her mother was unexpectedly stricken ill, and all of Jane's plans were thrown awry. While her mother was in the hospital, Jane undertook the responsibilities of the household. Fatie helped in many ways during her weekend visits.

Saddened by the thought of how little of life she had shared with her mother, Jane set about to make the days go as cheerfully as possible. Her father was outwardly calm and thoughtful as always, but Jane knew that his personal suffering was intense. Her parents had really loved and cared for each other throughout their marriage. Everyone was glad when Jane's mother was able to come home again. One evening at the dinner table, Jane told her, "You probably saved me from being a crook, Mother!"

"Well," her father responded in similar good-natured repartee, "maybe there're some blessings we've failed to count."

"What are you talking about, dear?" her mother asked in delight.

"Well," said Jane with a teasing smile, "remember when it was my job to see that Jed and Nat got to and from school, and you'd give me money for my fare on the street cars?"

Her parents nodded in acknowledgement.

"Well, do you remember how much I liked gum and those long licorice strands?"

"Oh, Jane," her mother laughed, "those rubbery old things you hung around your neck!"

"Yum," said Jane, remembering her sweet tooth, "they were delicious!"

"So?" her father asked, "where's our young crook?"

"Well," Jane replied with a broad smile, "sometimes I'd make the boys walk to school so I could use my carfare money to buy candy and gum. I'd share it with them and they'd promise not to tell. But fortunately mother found me out and explained all about learning to tell the truth. It's a good thing you made the point when I was young—no telling how I might have dealt with money and truth otherwise."

They all laughed and then Jane added, "You know, the Iranians have a proverb—'Conceal thy gold, thy destination and thy creed.' So pretense and misstatement, "tagiyeh," are common among them. In fact, their poet, Sa'adi, wrote that 'well-meaning falsehoods are better than a truth which leads to a quarrel.' Of course, we call this 'telling white lies.'"

While Jane was at home with her parents, she heard regularly from Akhtar, her loyal assistant in Iran. Akhtar was carrying on the daily English classes for the wealthy and the weekly meetings for the poor mothers. Akhtar reported that the location for the mothers' meetings had been moved from the quarters in central Tehran to a vacant building on the Mission Compound. This change made it easier for the missionary wives who were the teachers. Meanwhile, Akhtar and the Mission personnel began searching for a new site while still temporarily housing some of the classes in a small rental. The Presbyterian Board had granted proceeds from the sale of the Sage College property[1] to the Iran Bethel Project which, from 1940, was known as the Doolittle Project.

When Jane's mother showed very encouraging signs of recovery, Jane felt that she really must return to her duties in Iran, and did so. However, in October, 1948, just one month after she'd left home, Jane received word of her mother's death. She was deeply grieved. Despite her sorrow, Jane quietly pursued the tasks before her. She was fully persuaded that she was where God wanted her to be. This was proved to her again very soon.

Having operated in rental facilities for eight years, the Doolittle Project[2] purchased property off Sa'di Avenue. In February, 1949, the Project officially moved into the new quarters and continued its education program, using English as the language of instruction.

One of the faithful workers who served Jane for many years was Matavose, the custodian in charge of all the rental locations. When Iran Bethel was planning its move into new quarters, Jane realized that there was more work than Matavose could do. Soon after, the Lord brought Ibrahim, a fine young Turkish man from

Azarbaijan (northeastern Iran), to Jane's attention. Ibrahim was a village boy in a small town near Ardebil at the outbreak of the war in Iran. He had come to Tehran looking for work and was soon employed by the American Army. When the war ended, Ibrahim was without a job. Jane heard about him and he then took up quarters and work at Iran Bethel.

Soon after he began his new job, Ibrahim asked leave to go to his native village and bring back his betrothed, a girl of fourteen. When the couple returned, they first lived in a cellar room until their quarters in the southwest corner of the property were completed. When Jane asked Ibrahim the name of his wife, he said he did not know. This was undoubtedly true, as a man never spoke of his wife except as "the house" or "the mother of so and so." A fine, reliable worker, Ibrahim not only kept the school clean, but took care of many errands which took him throughout the city. Jane, having purchased a car to use for all the personal visits she made to the homes of the sick and needy, decided to send Ibrahim to driving school. For years thereafter he served as official driver for both the school and Jane.

When his wife, Mahsoltan, became pregnant, Jane sent her regularly to the nearby Women's Hospital for checkups. When the labor pains began, Jane sent her to the hospital. The hospital staff instructed her to go home and return in two weeks because "her time was not yet." However, the pains continued. Jane and Golebehar sent her back to the hospital again that night, but the staff said there was no doctor on duty and she should come back in the morning. However, around 2:00 A.M. one of the young children whom the women had taken into their home came running upstairs to the porch where Jane and Gertrude were sleeping. "Come quickly! Golebehar says the baby is here!"

Jane dashed down to the garden and found Mahsoltan on the cement floor of their little yard. Golebehar was kneeling close beside her, holding a baby girl. "Go quickly and get some colored string and scissors," instructed Golebehar. Jane did so. They then cut and tied the umbilical cord and sent the new mother to her room upstairs. Golebehar and Jane washed and clothed the infant, and according to custom, Golebehar stuck a small cloth containing a special ointment into the baby's mouth (to clean the baby's system).

Initiation into fatherhood had been the most frightening rite that Ibrahim had ever experienced. "Golebehar," he had asked in anxiety, "do all women cry out so loud, or is this just my wife?"

"No, no," Golebehar had comforted him, "it is the same for all women."

In the course of the years, the couple had five more children,"all healthy, beautiful and intelligent," comments Jane with pride in these members of "her" family.

With the enlarged quarters, Jane was able to open a clinic for the poor women who had continued to come to the "Wednesday meeting". During the course of the years, the sick made their way to this place of care and concern. But women with other problems also regularly came. Some were widows with little children; others had husbands who were addicted to opium. Still other women came to the clinic because their husband was in prison or in the hospital or just unwilling to exert himself to support the family. Some came because they were old and unable to work. Many of the young mothers who visited the clinic needed to learn about cleanliness. They were taught how to care for their infants, including the necessity of doing away with the swaddling clothes in which babies were sometimes kept for hours on end.

The needs among Iran's less fortunate never lessened. In fact, the needs only became more apparent as internal turmoil increased. Jane was constantly endeavoring to find ways to stimulate and provide more assistance to the many who came to the clinic for help. She knew that these represented only the smallest fraction of those in need. Jane considered it important to help as many as possible.

Each day, Jane sought the will of God in her life and in the work He had given her to do. She faithfully presented the needs of the poor to all whom she encountered, whether they were Muslim, Christian, Zoroastrian or Jewish. Those who could help were encouraged to do so in ways possible for them and through the passing years the work continued to expand.

The last several years had been a time of change for both Iran and Jane. However, 1951 would bring Jane another personal encounter with change.

NOTES

1. Although the Sage College property had appreciated enormously in value since its original purchase, the Iranian government reimbursed the Mission Board for the initial property costs when it took over the schools in 1940. The government used the dormitory building as a high school (which most of the Nurbakhsh students attended). The government eventually constructed a new building on the east side of the property and moved the high school there. Later, they razed the dormitory and built a beautiful opera house in its place. The opera house was named Rudaki Hall in honor of Rudaki (A.D. 919-943), recognized as the father of Persian poetry. Along with many hundreds of thousands of Iranians, Jane enjoyed attending special events at Rudaki Hall; but it was always with a small private tug-at-the-heart as she remembered the past. However, as Rudaki, who had died in great personal grief, had said: "What is past is past. Why persist in your sorrows? "

2. Being a very modest person, Jane preferred that the Doolittle Project go by the name of the Iran Bethel Project.

Part III

Where Goes That Dream
I Once Beheld?

CHAPTER NINE

Shadows and Light

"F ather critically ill. Can you come?" cabled Catherine.

Of course Jane would return home; everyone at the school and clinic assured her that they could manage without her for a time. Jane packed quickly and, for the first time in her life, made a speedy twenty-hour journey from Tehran to home, flying via Switzerland to London and then New York.

Since her mother's death, Jane's father had been living alone, cared for by a fine black woman, Sarah, whom Jane had employed for her parents before leaving New York in 1948. At that time, she had also arranged with the Presbyterian Board for furloughs every three years so as to be more accessible to her family. Catherine lived in Bronxville, New York, near enough to visit her father several times a week. At present, however, Catherine was exhausted from her care of him.

As soon as Jane arrived, Catherine and her husband took a much needed two-week rest at Cape Cod. As Jane cared for her father, she soon realized that he needed more expert medical care. After Catherine and Howard's return, they agreed together that a change of doctors was necessary and Mr. Doolittle was admitted to the Doctor's Hospital in New York City. Jane went there daily to be with him. For the last two weeks of his life she lived in the the hospital's hotel facilities for families. When he died, Jane found comfort repeating favorite lines to herself:

I need Thee, Oh, I need Thee
Every hour I need Thee.

and

Drop Thy still dews of quietness
Till all our striving cease.
Take from our souls the strain and stress
And let our ordered lives confess
The beauty of Thy peace.

Her father had been a gifted, loving man-of-God who had faithfully served out his earthly mission. He would now join his dear wife and young son, Nat, in heavenly reunion. It was his time to receive God's welcome blessing: " . . . well done, thou good and faithful servant" (Matthew 25:21).

When she returned to Yonkers, the family home seemed almost unreal, it was so quiet: no laughter; no probing questions; no fresh flowers from her father's garden. The green houseplants stood tall and straight as if on duty in a holding pattern. Indeed, everything seemed to be in a state of suspension. For the first time, Jane realized that home would no longer be a house in Westchester County, New York. From now on, home would be a memory in her heart.

Climbing the carpeted stairs to her second floor bedroom that afternoon in 1951, Jane recalled the day when, as a seventeen year old girl, she had come home from Capen to tell her parents that she wanted to be a missionary doctor in Africa. At Capen, she and her roommate Polly, and Polly's mother, had often prayed together and talked about God's call and one's responsibility toward non-Christians. Jane could still hear her father's response: "Then you must go to college! A missionary must have a college education." This had been something of a concession on his part as he hadn't been overkeen on the idea of "higher education" for women. Although, unbeknown to her, he had been investigating colleges already. Together, she and her father had climbed these stairs into her room. Kneeling beside Jane's bed, her father had earnestly petitioned God for His guidance and will in Jane's life. "That was more than thirty years ago," mused Jane.

Shortly thereafter, her father had made arrangements with the Capen School to completely change Jane's course of study. She would complete the English, History, Math, Science and Latin required for college entrance. It had meant hard work, for it all had to be mastered by June so Jane could take the Regent's examination. Since the four years of Latin could not be completed in such a short time, Jane had spent most of that following summer being tutored in Caesar, Cicero and Virgil. By the fall of 1917, Jane was able to complete the tests and enter Wells College as a freshman.

Standing alone in their home now, Jane realized how lonely her father must have been the three years since her mother's death, even with Catherine's visits. Her cousin, Amanda, had been a good friend to both Jane and her father, and had come to visit Mr. Doolittle from her home in Philadelphia. She had told Jane how, one day when she arrived, Mr. Doolittle had just finished writing Jane her weekly letter. "Who will write to Jane when I am gone?" he had wondered aloud as he sealed the envelope. "I will, Uncle Orrin," Amanda had responded. It was a promise Amanda would keep.

Amanda's mother, Laura, was an invalid due to a fall that had injured her spine, making it impossible to walk. When Laura had heard about Jane's first spinal operation, she had been greatly concerned that Jane, too, might never walk again. One of Laura's favorite stories was about the time when, as children, she and her sister, Grace, Jane's mother, had helped pack a missionary barrel. Grace had put her dearest doll into the trunk to send to the mission field. Laura used to wonder, "Was this an omen of the years to come?"

After largely dismantling the old family home, Jane returned to Tehran in 1952. More than ever, Iran was now her home. Shortly thereafter she bought an old residence situated within a block of Iran Bethel and made it home. From there, she quietly and conscientiously carried on the constantly increasing work. More and more people were coming to the clinic for help.

Jane received an unexpected pleasure the following year: Catherine and husband, Howard, came to visit her in Iran for three weeks. For them it was a revelation. Jane took them south to Isfahan and Shiraz, shrines of some of Iran's great poets; and to see some amazing relics of history. Then they went north to the Caspian Sea, to Rasht and Pahlevi where the climate is so different. Here, instead of bare mountains the slopes are covered with beautiful forests and the area is filled with rice paddies and tea plantations.

Jane and Catherine had never been overly congenial as children. Catherine was a pretty, sociable, artistic person, keen on following the latest fashion trends in clothing and make-up. Her parents had sent her to the best art schools in New York and Paris and she had returned to teach art in Des Moines, Iowa, and later, Millbrook, New York. Millbrook had been her home for many years and the sisters hadn't seen each other very often. But now, as adults, they were having a chance to appreciate each other.

Catherine was amazed to see some of the beneficial results of her younger sister's organizational ability. She observed Jane capably handle varying situations: the unexpected arrival of a government inspector; a visit with women of the aristocracy; the urgent pleas of some poor peasant women. Catherine was also impressed by what she heard from others about Jane. One of the highlights of her stay in Tehran was hearing Ruth Harman's tale about the time Ruth accompanied Jane on her regular Sunday visit to an elderly lady. The woman was a princess from the previous dynasty who had become a Christian. "What a fascinating lady the princess was!" Ruth had commented while relating the story:

> Except for two women servants, the princess lived all alone in a little house. She received Jane and me, as she lived, in the old style of life, sitting on large cushions on the floor. While we were there, the princess asked Jane to pray for a male heir for the shah.[1] Jane did so. I wondered what the shah would think if he could see Jane, the American missionary, praying for an heir for him at the request of a princess from a dynasty his father had overthrown! I think he would have been as impressed as I.

When the princess died, her Muslim relatives (most of whom lived in France) gave the woman a Muslim funeral in a Muslim cemetery. A few days after the funeral, Jane went alone to the new gravesite to read Scripture and pray for her Christian friend.

During Catherine and Howard's 1953 visit, Iran was divided over great political and economic concerns, including the nationalization of oil and activities involving Mossadegh and the shah. Catherine and Howard could sense the tension around them. They had asked on one occasion, "Isn't it nerve-racking to live in a country that always seems to be in turmoil and upset? Aren't you afraid?"

"No," Jane answered promptly and quietly. "I am not afraid. I just wish you could know all the fine people I know. I love them."

As Catherine and Howard were leaving, he said thoughtfully, "Thank you, Jane, for sharing yourself and your time with us. You've given us rich memories of these people and your work here." Catherine added, "It's been wonderful to have this time with you!"

Two years later, in 1955, a new time of sadness came into Jane's life with the death of faithful Golebehar. Jane derived some comfort from the fact that, at long last, Golebehar was free from the months of intense pain which cancer had inflicted. Still, Jane missed her loyal, devoted friend very deeply. The two had shared many experiences.

There had been the time when Golebehar rescued two of their houseguests from near asphyxiation. The friends, a mother and young daughter, were visiting Jane after a very dusty and trying overland trip from Mashad to Tehran. They wanted to freshen up and had gone to the bathroom located out in the garden. Wash water was heated by a large charcoal samovar in the bathroom. On this particular occasion, the charcoal hadn't been sufficiently burned off and was releasing monoxide gas. In the small, steam-filled room, the two were soon feeling very ill. By superhuman effort they managed to get the door pushed open and walked back to their rooms. There they collapsed across the bed. Golebehar had hurried in with vinegar to help revive them, and then brought hot tea.

Jane will always think of Golebehar fondly:

Golebehar was a jewel and thought of my every need. Although she did not become a Christian, she was most particular about our saying grace at meals. If one of us would start eating before it was said, she protested. If during the course of a day rain developed and she knew that I had not taken my umbrella, she would collect my rubbers and raincoat, put on her chador, and plod the half mile to the school to give them to me. Of course, she would get well soaked herself as Iranian women could not use umbrellas while dressed in their enveloping chador. For a couple of years after the school was closed in 1940, we kept two or three poor little girls in our home and it was Golebehar who cared for them.

Later that same year, Catherine's husband, Howard, died suddenly of a heart attack. The following spring, Jane received word that Catherine was to have a mastectomy, and Jane returned to the States to spend a month with her sister.

While together, the two women planned that Catherine would return to Iran to assist in Jane's school. So, beginning in 1957, Catherine spent seven months sharing her artistic talents with the Iran Bethel girls. This was a warm and wonderful experience for the two sisters. On her next furlough in 1958, Jane spent the weekends with Catherine in Chappaqua, traveling there from Columbia University.

With the many errands and schedules to meet in New York, Jane decided to learn to drive a car. She took lessons in Brooklyn and relished the unexpected sense of freedom that came with this accomplishment. Now she could, in a minor way, understand the almost delirious joy which affected Iranians when they came into possession of such a powerful, mechanized marvel.

Toward the end of the furlough, Gertrude came from London for a visit and Catherine arranged a two-month trip for all of them to Florida. Soon after their return and Gertrude's departure for England, Catherine's cancer returned. Jane decided she must remain in the States to care for her sister. While driving together to say goodbye to their brother, Jed, and his wife, Molly, Catherine collapsed. With great difficulty they drove back to Chappaqua and Catherine was immediately hospitalized. After several days she was able to return home and Jane cared for her there.

One day in December of 1959, a friend came in to relieve Jane of her constant bedside watch. Jane was resting and had just about dozed off when the friend hurried in. "So sorry to waken you but Catherine insists on seeing you right now!" Jane went in immediately and leaned over her sister to hear her last words: "I want you to tell everyone—everyone—that I think your work is the most wonderful in the world, the greatest means of bringing understanding and peace among nations. Tell—everyone!" A few days later Catherine slipped quietly away. Jane was grateful that God had granted such a wonderful benediction to their relationship.

Within a few short years Jane had lost her brother, Nat, her mother, her father, her brother-in-law and Catherine. Then, in October 1961, death also claimed Jane's brother, Jed, stricken during his sleep by a massive heart attack and Jane was saddened anew. "How ironic," she thought. "I was the frailest of the family. Now every single one of them is gone."

Jane was scheduled to retire from the Mission in 1964; however, the Mission Board did not have a replacement and asked Jane to continue. She agreed to do so until her successor was found. That was the same year a Muslim clergyman named Khomeini was officially "invited" to retire from his religious services to the Muslims of Iran. He took up exile, first in Turkey, then Iraq, and later in France. That year, however, Jane was not aware of this event or of the great impact it would one day have upon her life. Nor was she aware that in the United States a Hollywood actor named Ronald Reagan made a speech about America and its future that would ultimately bring worldwide consequences. Jane was quietly continuing her work at Iran Bethel and the clinic, constantly striving to demonstrate God's unconditional love for the people.

Meanwhile, the shah continued to vigorously try to change thousands of years of traditions. The goal was a revitalized, reunited land, that would surpass even the glories of Persia under the Aechaemenian kingships of Cyrus and Darius. Wanting his people to experience the twentieth century with its advancing technology, space achievements and labor-saving machinery, the shah instituted programs of major reform and reorganization. Consequently, Iranians found themselves in life-altering situations. This brought hope, joy and new purpose to some. But to others it brought dismay, anger and the festering of revengeful plans and desires.

For Iran's women it was a period of renewed hope. Previously, women had been legally classified with lunatics and criminals. Article 10 of the Iranian Electoral Law had stated:

> The following are legally barred from voting: women; those who are not legally able and are under guardianship; the bankrupt; the insane; beggars and those who earn their living by dishonorable means; criminals; thieves and other wrongdoers

who have violated the Islamic laws.

But in 1963, Iranian women were given the right to vote for the first time.

In addition to equal and universal suffrage for women, the government organized an educational corps—men and women military conscripts assigned to help supervise the building of schools in villages. The government also organized a health corps to examine the health needs of villagers, especially among children. Many other programs were designed to improve the conditions for all people, but women, especially, benefited. In 1966, all organizations for women were united into one central group under the leadership and patronage of Princess Ashraf, the shah's twin sister.

However, there were also powerful mullahs who resolutely and actively opposed education for women for fear of losing their hold on the people. Indeed, patterns of male domination had existed in the Middle East long before Islam. The custom of veiling had been practiced in Palmyra in the first century A.D. and in the Byzantine empire, and other nearby areas, long before Muhammad. Muslim converts continued this pattern, interpreting certain passages from the Quran as being supportive of it.

Jane always sought to do her best to show the women of Iran that God considered them persons of equal worth with men. She did so, not in a way that would interfere with their roles and responsibilities as wives and mothers, but in a way that would enhance their lives, giving them greater opportunities to serve their families and their country. Many of the students who received their education at Iran Bethel and Sage College repaid all that had been done for them by giving of their time, talents and resources to help their own people.

In May of 1966, Jane's replacement, Dr. Frances Gray, arrived.[3] In the change of leadership it was decided that the work among the poor had to be closed. At that time there were more than 10,000 people who had been assisted in the clinic. Some of the Iran Bethel alumnae who had helped in the clinic were distressed to learn that this work would cease. They got busy and raised enough money to buy a small place so that the clinic could continue, and it reopened in its new location not far from Iran

Bethel in August, 1966.

Jane intended to continue her work at the clinic, but first she wanted to return to the United States for a visit. Before she left, her former students and friends wanted to honor her. They knew that the Ministry of Education was planning a party in honor of her outstanding educational service in Iran, so the president of the Iran Bethel Alumnae Association contacted the ministry and told them that the alumnae wanted to give the party. She explained that in addition to the government officials and dignitaries, there were many others the alumnae wanted to invite. But the ministry said no, they wanted to give the party. However, the ministry told the alumnae they could invite anyone they wanted to include. So, a joyous party was held for Jane in the gardens of the Ministry of Education and she was given a special medal for her service.

During this period in her life, Jane received many honors and tributes from those who knew and appreciated her work in Iran. The Commodore Fishers, missionaries posted in Hamadan in 1921, remembered meeting Jane on her very first journey into Iran.

> So well we remember her as a sweet, lovely, very young lady on her way to Tehran. Little did we dream then that we were meeting and seeing for the first time the woman who would come to bless and influence more women in Iran, for more years, than anyone will ever know. She trained the head, the heart and hands of so many. She had the rare faculty of expecting the best in others—because she gave her best. She is very understanding—she inspired in her students the desire to be of service, training them to the meaning of serving others in her clinic work—the real beginning of social service in Tehran . . . .

The late Reverend Dr. John Elder,[4] another of the dedicated missionaries serving in Iran, wrote and presented the following tribute to Jane at the Mission party given in honor of her retirement.

TRIBUTE TO JANE DOOLITTLE

MAY 1966

> To remember Jane Doolittle is
> To remember a reverent, well-disciplined student body whom it was always a privilege to address.
> To remember successive commencement exercises that combined

happiness and tears, smoothness and spontaneity, warmth and reverence.

To remember teachers' conferences, organized to the last detail, yet so unobtrusively that one had to look to see it was there.

To remember a summer home where every tired and overworked colleague and friend could find unfailing hospitality and renewal.

To remember one who could "see the things you've given-your-life-to" broken, yet could stoop to build them up again with worn-out tools.

To remember one who, despite a thousand clamoring duties, for many years never failed her weekly visits to a shut-in church member living ten miles away in Shemiran.

To remember one who enriched our church schools everywhere with her carefully worked-out courses in Bible and ethics.

To remember one who taught successive generations of often spoiled and self-centered girls to work for and think of others less fortunate.

To remember one who has helped train a significant proportion of the leaders of women in changing Iran.

To remember one who never permitted pain or physical discomfort to divert her in any measure from her accepted calling.

To remember one whom a long-time assistant and colleague characterized as being the "perfect school principal."

May the "last of life for which the first was made" be the finest and happiest of all.

After a visit to the U.S., Jane returned to Iran in 1967 to participate in the official inauguration ceremonies for the Doolittle Clinic. One of the hostesses was Madame Farideh Diba (the mother of the Empress, two of whose aunts had been graduated from Iran Bethel).

That same year, the whole country participated in the coronation of the shah. Although Mohammad Reza Pahlavi had assumed his leadership role as shah when he was twenty-two, it was not until his forty-eighth birthday (October 26, 1967) that he and the people celebrated his coronation with ceremonies, festivities and parades.

As with his father, the Golestan Palace was again the site for the crowning. The shah used the same emerald and diamond crown as had his father, also placing it on his own head. However, he shared the glory of the occasion with his beautiful young empress, Farah Diba, aged twenty-nine, upon whose head he placed a spectacular jewelled crown. The shah changed royal tradition so that, in the event of his death before the crown prince reached maturity (age twenty-one), the empress could rule as regent in her own right. A week's celebration followed and the first event was the opening of the new Rudaki Hall—erected on the former Sage College property where Jane had once lived.

The following year, 1968, Jane received another honor. Wells College was celebrating its 100th anniversary[5] and chose to give awards to ten of its most outstanding graduates. Jane, selected as one of these, decided to make a special trip home. She was pleased to have the opportunity to remind the women of the original purpose of "Wells in Persia": to go in Christian love to share their training and expertise in service to others. At the ceremony she briefly commented:

> . . . I wish each of you could see first-hand some of the fine re-
> sults of your several years of financial support, participation
> and interest in all we've undertaken. May God be honored.
> And thank you all again for your part in these efforts.

Jane's cousin, Amanda, attended this event with her husband, Russell Craig. Amanda's mother, Laura Ferguson, had also been a graduate of Wells College (class of 1884).

Returning to Iran after this brief interlude, Jane continued her endeavors. She was increasingly proud of the fact that "the work of the Doolittle Clinic was primarily done by the alumnae of Iran Bethel and Sage College."

Those coming to the Doolittle Clinic needed help, information and encouragement. The babies needed milk, so the clinic staff and volunteers taught the young mothers how to measure and mix the dry ingredients. These were provided by the Ministry of Health to supplement the mothers' own meager supply. Some of the Iran Bethel alumnae established a literacy program. Regular classes were held for the women who came to the meetings at the clinic, and certificates were given to those who finished the fourth class. A team of alumnae also went to an elementary school in south Tehran to provide a 10:00 A.M. nutrition snack for the children. To demonstrate the need for cleanliness and or- derliness, the alumnae would carefully wash and dry each drink- ing glass in the presence of the school's teachers and students.

One of the mother's who came to the clinic for help was Par- vin. This young woman, her husband and their family of seven children, had a little shop from which they sold groceries. At the back of it was limited space for a courtyard which contained a toilet, a tiny pool of water, and one cramped room where the entire family lived day and night. Her husband, Hassan, had built this compound for them far outside the city limits during the years when he suffered from tuberculosis. However, he had no title deed for it. Hassan died in 1968 and Parvin had to carry on alone. She wanted to sell the place, but couldn't because of the lack of any deed. Parvin struggled to earn a living from the shop while the Clinic clothed the children and otherwise did what it could to help. In spite of their poverty, whenever Jane came to visit them one of the children would run into the shop, open the refrigerator and get a bottle of Pepsi for her—a hospitable gesture that Jane had found to be so characteristic of Iranians.

When an American friend came to see Jane in Iran, the visits to the Doolittle Clinic were the highlight of her stay. She remembers that:

> The care and devotion to all the little children and their mothers, with no thought of whether they were Christians, was a blessed sight; as were the Thursday afternoons when the poor mothers in their chadors came and Jane talked with them. All had grave and serious problems—husbands who were alcoholics or on drugs; little children in need of milk, mothers needing cooking oil.
>
> When we traveled around Tehran, people of all ages would stop and greet her, but especially the poor women who would have kissed her hand had she allowed. These expressions of joy and reverence, and Jane's responses, were beautiful to see.

Even with the economic boom of the early 1970s, the number of poor in the capital city kept increasing. Many villagers, weary from heavy agricultural labor and the scarcity of financial support in the villages, believed that Tehran was Utopia. They poured into the area looking for well-paying job opportunities. The government tried to cope with the imperatives of this migration by providing temporary housing. Tents were erected in the southern part of the city in an area hidden behind high walls so that the general public wouldn't notice. (A plan was also under way for constructing new housing to sell to the poor. This plan envisioned the purchasers paying 3,000 rials ($43.00) a month for fifteen years, and then the dwelling would become theirs. This was a great deal of money for the very poor, though the plan was helpful to others.)

Jane walked about the tent cities, and among all the poor, un-afraid. There might be thieves and criminals living there, but she "always felt that it was the Lord's work and that He would take care of me. He did. I never had any qualms about being with these people."

The city's problems were enormous, and although the work of the Doolittle Clinic was limited, it was welcomed and received with appreciation, both by the poor and by the government authorities. Jane frequently praised God when she thought about the work of former students. Although almsgiving is one of the five pillars of Islam,[6] the alumnae's responsiveness to the poor in sharing of their time, energy and material resources all went far beyond Islamic law. Their deeds came in the name of the God of love whom Jane served.

NOTES

1. Both Queen Fawzia and Queen Soroya had been divorced for failing to provide the shah with a male heir. It was Queen Farah, the shah's third (and last) wife, who bore him two sons and two daughters.

2. Muhammad had set forth the legitimacy of marrying four wives, and Muslim societies tend to be made up almost exclusively of the married. By age twenty to twenty-five there are few single women who have never been married. Widows or divorced women are to be remarried to men who already have at least one wife. Absolute fidelity is demanded of wives, whether the marriage relationship is polygamous or monogamous.

3. Three years after Dr. Gray arrived, Iran Bethel became Damavand College, an English-speaking, four-year college for women. The Iran Bethel facilities were used until new buildings were constructed for the college in a finer area outside the city.

4. Dr. John Elder served in Iran from 1922-1964 as a missionary with the United Presbyterian Church. His published scholarly works include eleven books in Persian and two in English. He authored many articles and assisted in the preparation of courses for Leadership Instruction and Training International, in Houston Texas. Dr. Elder died on Sept. 3, 1981.

5. Wells College, in Aurora, New York, was one of the first women's colleges in the United States. It was founded in 1868 by Henry Wells of Wells Fargo fame. Henry Wells was the son of a Presbyterian minister. His two brothers went into the ministry and it is likely that Henry would also have chosen this profession save for the fact that he was a stammerer and was unable to overcome this speech problem. However, he saw the need for a good, reliable express service and established the first private delivery service in the United States. In 1852, he and William G. Fargo founded Wells, Fargo and Company which became one of the most powerful firms in the western states. In addition to carrying passengers, freight and mail, they also developed a banking business on the Pacific Coast. In 1918, Wells Fargo merged with six other express companies to form the American Railway Express. The story is told that one day when Henry Wells was traveling in Philadelphia, he observed a college for women being constructed. He is said to have declared: "I'd rather do something like that than be president of the United States." Wells was a business associate and friend of Ezra Cornell, who founded Cornell University in 1865. In 1866, Cornell invited Wells to establish his "Wells female department" on the Cornell property and to share the facilities, libraries and museums available there.

After due consideration, Wells continued with his original plan to establish and maintain a small college for women. The Founder's Address, delivered at the laying of the cornerstone on July 19, 1867, included this comment: deemed proper to hold woman in a condition of mental inferiority and to withhold from her the educational privileges which were freely accessible to the other sex. As yet, however, facilities for her systematic and thorough instruction are but scantily supplied. Wells College continues to maintain its high standards and chooses to keep its enrollment limited and to women only. In tribute to Wells memory, Wells College graduating seniors ride to their annual commencement in a Wells Fargo stagecoach. Today, seven colleges and universities are within a half hour of the Wells campus.

6. According to Islamic law, one-fifth ("khoms") and one-tenth ("zakat") of one's income are to be given to the poor or for religious causes.

The Bending Cypress

Jane, along with millions worldwide, was thrilled on June 20, 1969, by the accomplishments of the American astronauts, the first humans ever to walk on the moon. This thrilling triumph stirred the imaginations and hopes of people everywhere.

The shah, ever searching for ways to stir the hearts and minds of his people, pondered a new question. Wouldn't a celebration of Iran's ancient and noble history serve as a perfect medium for strengthening a deeper sense of national identity and pride? And so, for more than two years thereafter, Iran's most gifted and creative talent worked on this dramatic project. With the celebration, Iran came to world attention as broad media coverage allowed viewers and readers to glimpse a modern Iranian pageant. News briefs, such as the following, poured forth:

Persepolis, October 1971

Here at Persepolis, amid the ruins of the great palace that monarch King Darius and his son, King Xerxes, constructed more than 2000 years ago, Persia/Iran celebrated its 2500 anniversary.

In spectacular Persian grandeur and glory a four-day party was held with officials hosting top-ranking VIPs from 69 nations who came to share in the festivities. These distinguished men and women were royally-housed in a specially created and designed Tent City on a nearby 60-acre plot.

The event served as a salute to the shah's 30-year reign as well as to the anniversary of the founding of the world's first great empire.

Throughout the celebration, Jane marvelled at the artistic talents of the Iranians who mingled fact and fiction from their national mythology into an engrossing live-action socio-historical drama. It was both impressive and unforgettable.

As Jane's busy, but routine, days rolled on, October 28th brought her to the startling realization that she'd been in Iran for fifty years! Was she really that twenty-two year old girl who'd arrived here a stranger, alone and uncertain, so long ago? To commemorate these years of Jane's service, and as a way of raising additional funds for the Doolittle Clinic, the alumnae of Iran Bethel and Sage College planned a festive party to honor their beloved teacher and "angel mother." This joyous occasion came on February 10, 1972. Jane was not a star suddenly born—she'd been quietly sent by Heaven years ago to reflect God's light through her steady, constant outreach.

This night's celebration, starring Jane Doolittle, was like a Persian folktale with a wondrous splendor all its own. In the Ayra Sheraton Hotel, downstairs beneath the ballroom, white-jacketed waiters were hurrying around the curved buffet table to complete last minute arrangements. The maitre d' viewed the proceedings with his professional expertise, noting a few details which he promptly instructed the waiters to correct.

Jane felt like a spectator in a drama. She nodded and smiled to those within eye view. These were her "girls," her friends. Almost every woman in the place was a former student or the relative of a student. These were among those who had responded to the Christian love that Jane brought with her to Iran when she had accepted the three-year call to come to this land and teach in a Presbyterian mission school.

At the conclusion of the sumptuous buffet, the crowd moved upstairs to the ballroom. Wearing a simple black velvet gown, Jane, stately and poised, fell into step with their energetic pace. She wondered what the alumnae had planned for this part of their program. An exciting variety of pre-dinner activities and entertainment had already been offered for the delight of the 1,000 guests; now what was coming?

As soon as the people had seated themselves, a burst of applause interrupted Jane's thoughts. The Minister of Education, the first Iranian woman ever to hold that position,[1] walked to the podium. All eyes turned to her. Loudly and clearly she suddenly exclaimed, "Miss Doolittle, please come forward!"

Jane rose and mounted the few stairs to the platform. The women faced each other. The Minister smiled and shook hands with Jane. "In recognition of your fifty years of loving, dedicated and outstanding service to us," she said, "we have the privilege of bestowing upon you this gold medal," picking it up from the podium. "It is the highest educational award of our country!" As one, the audience rose to give Jane a standing ovation. Jane bowed her head in acknowledgement and gratitude as she received the honor.

"Oh God," Jane petitioned swiftly and silently, "give me the right words to say. May they know that everything I have done through these years has been Thy work, for Thy honor and glory, not mine." She wished her family were present.

Jane turned to the microphone: "When I came here fifty years ago, I was a stranger and did not know what to expect. Now I know you and love you. I know your great abilities and possibilities. It is written that ' . . . Unto whomsoever much is given, of him shall much be required . . . '(Luke 12:48b). You have much, so God expects much of you. What are you going to do with the remainder of your lives?" With an all-embracing smile and a deep bow, Jane returned to her seat, her mind awhirl with a lifetime of memories. The sound of their thunderous applause would echo in her heart forever. "To God be the glory."

As time added years to her life, Jane was becoming more aware of the great inconveniences in her old house. There were many stairs to climb; the kitchen was out in the yard; the street gate was some many feet from the house. With the death of their faithful old gate-keeper, the latter problem became more acute. What to do?

Jane had an opportunity to sell the half of her property containing the old house. On the remaining property she used the funds from the sale to build a small one-story, two-bedroom house with a den and modern conveniences—indoor plumbing, new appliances, central heating and air-conditioning. There was even a small room where Gertrude could display and sell her Persian character dolls. This was her way of raising money to help the poor and needy and an activity especially important to her since retirement. When they moved in on June 20, 1972, Jane and Gertrude expected to be able to live comfortably in this little piece of earthly paradise until God called them into His Heavenly paradise. Time would prove otherwise.

Often during the summer, the two women went to their cottage in the nearby mountains. This retreat provided them with a refreshing and welcome change from the noisy, crowded and dusty city. Robert and Carolyn Bucher, also missionaries, experienced renewal and cordial hospitality at this cottage:

> It was a bit of heaven to come an hour's drive to this cool village from the intense heat of Tehran and spend a day or weekend. Jane and Gertrude put up two or three tents so small families could camp there for a week or so during the hottest weather. And what wonderful walks we had as well as dips in the mountain stream, and what fun playing games!
>
> The service that was most unique was the Sunday A.M. worship time on Jane's front porch. Her Christian friends on either side of her cottage, and any others nearby (including) many non-Christians, were invited to attend. So about ten to twenty people would worship in song, prayer and discussion of the Bible. Jane was very faithful through the years with this service which was a real witness of her spiritual goal to her friends and neighbors.

In one of her letters from the cottage, Jane recounted that:

> . . . Yesterday morning our gardener here in the mountains showed us our healthy cucumber plants. Shortly after, a villager, who frequently visits us selling his wares, came to call and obtain Gertrude's usual help. As he left, he remarked to our gardener about our healthy plants—and within an hour the cucumber plants had shrivelled! Shokri came to us in wrath at our admitting a person who would thus cast the evil eye on our crops. It is difficult for us to comprehend the complete belief in the power of the evil eye which is still so prevalent here. Would that these fine people could come into an understanding of the freedom in Christ—freedom from superstition and fear—and the glory of the Risen Christ.

Every year the headmaster of the Tehran British School invited Jane to come and tell the students about the work of the clinic. The students wrote their varied impressions of her visit:

> The small old lady, thin and wrinkled,
> But surrounded by a glow of personality.

> Her thin white hair
> Scraped into a bun.
> Her mellow voice trembling with emotion
> Seems to explode as she tells us of the sorrow, sweat and
>   tears of unfortunate people.
> A grand old lady.

> Miss Doolittle got up and talked about the people at the clinic.
> She made you feel that you were not just giving a few tins of
> food. . . . She talked about the troubles of the poor people in
> Iran. One could, and some did last year, burst into tears. She
> was really a kind old woman. Once or twice I caught her glanc-
> ing at the food [the students had brought for the poor], smiling
> and looking thoughtful, probably thinking of the good it would
> do.

> Little in body, maybe, but in spirit, in courage, in kindliness,
> she is the exact opposite. All the things she has done are re-
> markable. She does not turn away from the poor and needy
> people. She does not walk away unconcerned. She, like the
> Good Samaritan, stops and helps them. By herself she has
> made people happy, and in doing that she is carrying out
> God's will. To me, and others, she is an angel.

As a follow-up to Jane's visit to the British school, the headmaster arranged a field trip for a group of his students to see the
work of the clinic. These students also recorded their impressions
of the visit:

> The ancient looking walls were brown and made of mud brick,
> with holes that had wasps living in them. A green door
> squeaked open, beyond was a courtyard which had a few fruit
> trees, a small pool and a path running around it.

> A small lady with a big heart came out of a door. Her white
> hair was pulled back from her wrinkled face. She had blue eyes
> [brown] which sparkled. Her voice trembled as she told us of
> some of the patients she had helped.

> The clinic had an aura of antiseptic cleanliness about it, not at
> all unpleasant. We walked around, looking in the rooms. Eve-
> rywhere there were Iranian women in their long flowing cha-
> dors. We saw all the different sections. We talked about the re-
> markable Miss Doolittle who has been in Iran for fifty years.
> We walked out knowing we would never forget our little trip.

The school nurse who accompanied the group of students was

also impressed:

> As we went through the oddly-shaped door, we could feel a
> strange atmosphere about the place. The women all around
> were chattering as we went in, but stopped abruptly when they
> saw us. All the rooms were very small, but they were very
> clean and tidy.
> As we looked around, it made me think of a World War I hos-
> pital. It made me think about all the battles. I looked into one of
> the rooms and saw a man with a bandage round his head—I al-
> most thought he was a wounded soldier. You almost expected
> to see biplanes locked in the combat of a dog-fight, or perhaps
> a wounded soldier in battle-dress being wheeled around. The
> clinic was incredibly clean. Although the patients looked clean,
> I was sure they all needed help.

Many who visited the clinic came away changed by what they
saw and experienced:

> I went in a school girl, came out a dreamer.
> She makes me feel humble, she makes me think.
> She makes me want to help.
> She makes me want to help everyone.
> My mind was a kaleidoscope of different sensations.
> And before I knew it we were back at school.

In July, 1973, Iran again became the center of world focus
when, after seventy-two years of foreign control of its oil industry, the government took over the management of its underground wealth. This event impacted upon the whole world in
significant ways. The alphabetical letters "B. O." and "A. O."
took on a powerful new meaning: Before Oil and After Oil. The
shah's White Revolution programs were carried forth more vigorously than ever after this change.

The shah was convinced that "women must contribute to the
modernization of the country by taking part in welfare and civic
functions . . . and help the . . . people of the country, especially
those in the thousands of villages and small towns."[2] In 1975, the
first year in the International Decade of Women, there were more
well-educated, professional Iranian women in service to their
country than at any time in preceding history. Women were
making outstanding contributions in medicine, law, science,
health, archaeology, psychology, administration, education, gov-

ernment, communications, business, the arts, sports, labor and agriculture. (The country's labor force had always included women as important workers in agriculture, factories, industry and home industry such as weaving.)

That same year, the shah created the Ministry of State for Women's Affairs and appointed a very capable Iranian woman to direct activities in behalf of improving conditions for women. The shah's twin sister, Princess Ashraf, actively supported the welfare and upgrading of the status of women.

> . . . Whether within the family, at school or at work, to be born a woman is to be handicapped in some way. Not only is this situation extremely unjust and contrary to fundamental human rights and human dignity, but its harmful repercussions also affect men and children just as much as women and severely hampers the social and economic progress of mankind.[3]

Illiteracy was high among women in Iran and so was a matter of grave concern. Girls married very young and immediately assumed heavy maternal, household and agricultural responsibilities. Princess Ashraf emphasized the importance of educating women with a saying:

> Educate a man and you educate a person.
> Educate a woman and you educate a nation.[4]

When Empress Farah, the shah's third and last wife, celebrated her 37th birthday on October 14, 1975, a four-page, color news supplement honoring her was entitled: "Farah As The Mother Of The Nation." Her own mother, Madame Farideh Diba, is said to have asked her only child:

> Are you going to be just another pretty face, another wife of a shah, another mother of a son, a prince, or are you going to do something yourself as a person, accept responsibilities and challenges, discover what you are capable of, and give a new image of women in Iran?[5]

These twentieth century aspirations may have recaptured the thirteenth century thoughts of Nasir al-din of Tusi, who wrote:

> Human beings need each other for their continued existence both as individuals and as a species: moreover, without continued existence they cannot attain perfection. Thus, the perfection, the completion, of each individual, depends on other individuals of the species . . . .[6]

Jane, continuing to depend upon God and other people to support her work, found the years bringing other changes of dramatic proportion. In 1976 the Iranian calendar was changed from the Muslim year, 1355, dating from the time of Muhammad, to the year 2535, to date from Cyrus the Great, first ruler of the Persian Empire (separation of church and state?). On March 21, 1977, Daylight Savings Time was adopted. At the same time it was decreed that shop hours become uniform. Shops were to open at 9 A.M. and close at 7 P.M. This distressed many shopkeepers and patrons. Shops had traditionally opened at dawn and closed after 8:00 or 9:00 P.M. in the evening.

In 1977, Jane was pleased to assist the committee in charge of revising the Persian translation of the New Testament. She found this endeavor most rewarding. Around Jane's house, tall buildings and apartment houses were continually being constructed. In contrast, her area was also filling with many small shops. In addition, there were concerns that the Ministry of Health was about to abolish all private clinics. Would the Doolittle Clinic be closed and end another area of Jane's lifelong service to Iran?

Hoping to safeguard the future of the clinic, the alumnae president contacted the doctor who headed the Cancer Institute. Could he take the clinic under his jurisdiction? This doctor had helped in the work of the Doolittle Clinic before resuming his final medical training in England. He was well-acquainted with the clinic, its purpose and program, and had even brought his cousin, the Empress, on a visit. In his current role, therefore, he was able to offer new guidelines and directions. In April 1977, the clinic expanded its hours of service to six full days a week. This enabled it to meet the needs of the increasing number of patients. The patrons were always asked to pay a small fee for service if possible (equivalent to about twenty-five cents). The fee helped to give the people a sense of dignity and responsibility.

The women of the American Women's Club were among those who became active supporters of Jane's work. The Club's newsletter reported that:

> The clinic she now administers reflects all her care and dedication. Inside the door is a bright sunny courtyard. The rooms are all freshly painted and spotless. A gynecologist and a pediatrician are on duty . . . . The clinic handles thousands of patients

a year, mostly from south Tehran.

Once a week clothing is distributed . . . . Much of this is what
you have donated . . . . It is desperately needed so always
think of her work when you check your closets each season . . .
    Before the annual No Ruz season, the AWC clubhouse be-
comes a collection depot for foodstuffs . . . . Staples such as
sugar, rice, flour and oil are taken to the clinic by an AWC Welfare Committee and distributed by Miss Doolittle to the people
in need about her . . . .

On the second floor of the clinic is a charming room, a children's library, all bright colors and lovely books. It was organized and decorated by an alumna of Iran Bethel School and is
open one day a week for the charge of one toman [about fifteen
cents] a year.

Jane was very proud of this latest activity at the clinic. One of
the alumnae had undertaken the circulating library project all on
her own. She'd papered the room, put in bookcases and loaded
them with books, and obtained a tape recorder and a small pro-
jector for the children's entertainment. The children came eagerly
every Monday afternoon to return their books, borrow new ones
and share in handicraft activities.

Ever mindful of her purpose and desire to be God's person in
His service, Jane frequently checked her focus. "And what of all
this has been useful for the advancement of the Kingdom?" she
would ponder. "'A thousand years in Thy sight are but as yesterday' . . . . God, I pray that somehow You will use to Your glory
whatever has been worthwhile." The answer came as a deep
sense of peace within her heart.

Throughout 1977 there were new rumblings and pressures
surfacing in Iran. A writer for the *Chicago Tribune* reported one
shadow in an October article entitled "No live and let lib in
Iran."

Women's liberation doesn't sit well with some Iranian men.
Two newspapers reported Tuesday that masked students
burned a bus and damaged three others and spread leaflets at
Tehran University warning coeds not to mix with male students . . . . The attack on the buses appeared aimed at frightening women away from travel in company with men. The newspapers . . . said the leaflets were the work of "black reaction,"
Shah Mohammad Reza Pahlavi's term for Islamic fanatics who

oppose women's emancipation. The Iranian monarch has been trying for some time to modernize his country's tradition-bound society.

From reading Jane's annual summer report for the year 1978, her friends and supporters might not gather that a major crisis was being fomented in Iran. (Indeed, some were predicitng that the fall of the shah was imminent!) Jane conscientiously endeavored to maintain her usual routine. She wrote of her continuing visits to the house-bound, of meetings with former students and friends, of distributing the donated clothing, food and money; and of clinic repairs. She also shared how she and Gertrude were cheered by Chippy, their dog, and the welcoming chirps of Jane's canaries. In closing she commented: "Each of the above adds to the joy of living! I praise God and thank you all."

But the heavy black shadows were increasingly ominous. The Prime Minister was executed. The Islamic Revolutionaries, under the leadership of Khomeini in France, were intensifying their program. The shah's Pahlavi Dynasty was under direct attack and 1979 brought accelerated political activity and cataclysmic changes.

On January 13 the shah selected a new Prime Minister to steady the country. Four days later, a grieving and ill shah, stricken with lymphatic cancer, agreed to leave Iran with his wife. (Their children had previously left.) On the first of February a triumphant Khomeini returned to Iran and received a tumultous welcome. By early April Khomeini's regime had established a new Islamic Repulic. Another Prime Minister was appointed. In November the United States Embassy was seized by Iranian militants and Iran again became the center of world attention.

It so happened that Jane and Gertrude had left Iran in early September to make one of their periodic journeys, leaving Ibrahim in temporary charge of their home and affairs in Tehran. Gertrude stopped in England to visit with relatives and Jane toured about the U.S., reconnecting with long-time friends and supporters. One stop for Jane was Miffletown, Pennsylvania, near Harrisburg. Jane had first visited Miffletown in 1950 when the Westminister Church began supporting her work. Mary Leeper, her hostess, remembers:

I was teaching the Junior Sunday School in 1950. Each Sunday
thereafter the children collected their coins to send to Miss
Doolittle for her mission work. She corresponded with us several times a year and her letters were always published in our
bulletin . . . . We were now overjoyed to have Miss Doolittle
visit us again. One of the most enjoyable aspects of her visit
was that, upon receiving our gift of $375 she immediately said,
"Oh, I will send this to the clinic in Tehran!" Somehow, that is a
monument to her and her work.

Another touching moment came when Jane was in our home . .
. . After dinner we turned on our TV and were watching
"Boomer," the story of a small dog who was really a friend to
man. After a while Jane spoke up and said, "I can hardly stand
to watch this, it makes me so homesick for my dog who is at
home in Tehran." We felt so sorry for her.

In spite of being homesick for Tehran, Jane's remaining weeks
in the States passed pleasantly. She was with retired missionaries
in California when news of the storming of the U.S. Embassy in
Tehran shocked the world. At first she thought it would be a
short-lived incident similar to a previous brief stand-off. However, soon Jane and the world became increasingly concerned as
the days dragged into long weeks and months of mounting
strain and tension.

In March, Gertrude, visiting in the eastern U.S., was getting
restless and anxious to get home to Tehran as soon as possible.
She felt they had been gone long enough. "Jane, can't we go
home now?" she wrote. "Please get our airline tickets at once!"
But something told Jane to wait—that by No Ruz on March 21
there would be convincing guidance as to what to do under these
uncertain circumstances.

While visiting her Cousin Amanda in Philadelphia, she received the first of three cables on March 19. It read: "Do not return to Iran you are blacklisted as a spy." Jane withheld this information from Gertrude until a few days later when the two
were reunited in New York, supposedly prior to their return
flight to Iran. Although their shock absorbers had had years of
testing, the two women were nonetheless stunned and grieved
by the last two similar messages:

"Do not return now, probably never!"
Jane's mind was numb and racing all at the same time. "I can't

go back. I won't ever see our comfortable little home in Tehran, built just right for our remaining years . . . no stairs to climb . . . so near the stores. What about our many friends who depend upon us for help and encouragement—the shut-ins, the young mothers, the children? Dear Ibrahim and Mahsoltan and their dear family. Will I never again enjoy our dog, my canaries, the car, the summer cottage? Oh, what will happen to all my mementos—the family pictures, the keepsakes, my cherished Wells College memory book. Iran is our home. Are we homeless?"

Jane could only fall back on her faith that a God of Love would reveal His plan in time:

> Hast thou not known? Hast thou not heard that the everlasting God, the Lord, the Creator of the ends of the earth, fainteth not neither is weary?—He giveth power to the faint, and to them that have no might He increaseth strength. Even the youths shall faint and be weary—but they that wait upon the Lord shall renew their strength; they shall run and not be weary; they shall walk and not faint (Isaiah 40: 28-31).

NOTES

1. The first woman Minister of Education was later executed by the Khomeini regime.

2. See Mohammad Reza Shah Pahlavi, *Mission for My Country*, London, Hutchinson, 1961.

3. See Princess Ashraf Pahlavi, *Faces In A Mirror, Memoirs from Exile*, Prentice Hall, Inc., 1980, p. 225.

4. Ibid, p. 227.

5. See Betty Friedan, "Coming Out of the Veil," *The Ladies Home Journal*, June 1975, p. 99.

6. See Nasir-al-din Tusi, *Bridge of Turquoise*, Roloff Beny, McClelland and Stewart, Limited, The Canadian Publishers, p. 118.

CHAPTER ELEVEN

Love Remembers

I ran continued to be a chief topic of international concern; the days were anxious and uncertain for many. The American hostages—what was happening to them? And what about the other Americans still in that country? People who knew Jane were concerned about her. What was she going to do?

Jane and Gertrude waited on the Lord in prayer, seeking the answers to their needs. Homelessness was a new and sobering experience. They moved about, lodging in a succession of hotels, motels, and inns, as well as staying with friends. But these one-night stands were very uncomfortable for both of them.

When Lois Osborn, a friend from college days, heard that Jane was stranded in the U.S. with only two suitcases, a coat and a handbag, she shared this information with other friends in her town. Within a matter of weeks, a concerted response to Jane's situation came from a collection of college friends and church and community people, most of them strangers.

On June 2, 1980, Jane and Gertrude were driven from Rhode Island to the small picturesque town of Cortland, New York, just ninety miles from Wells College. There the homeless wanderers were cordially welcomed into a centrally-located "half-a-house" (duplex) which had been newly painted and totally furnished. Looking about this fine temporary-residence-in-the-U.S., Jane was amazed, once again, at how God demonstrates His love!

Every room in the three-bedroom duplex was attractively and meticulously furnished. Jane's college friends had taken special care to find a tall-backed, well-cushioned rocking chair which would comfortably support her back. She was very grateful for

this as she still wore the kind of back brace that Dr. Hibbs had
prescribed many years ago. There was also a long, firm daven-
port that she could rest on during the day instead of climbing the
stairs to the bedroom on the second floor. The good desk, chair
and typewriter would make it possible for her to continue her
long-neglected correspondence. The pantry was full of food; the
sunny kitchen was well-equipped. And to Gertrude's great joy
there was a piano and an outside garden.

As they settled into their new home, the accounts of the exiled
shah's death in Egypt brought the critical issues of Iran into
sharp focus again. Charlotte and Herrick Young, thankful to
know Jane's whereabouts, forwarded a copy of a letter recently
received from one of the few remaining American teachers:

> Although we have been able to keep our school thus far, things
> are increasingly unpromising. After numerous restrictive steps,
> it is now clear that licenses for all international and private
> schools will lapse this month. The government plans to oper-
> ate, as a government school, one large international school in
> three languages (French, German and English) with separate
> campuses for girls and boys. Our school will become the boys'
> English language international school.
>
> We are complimented that our international program is to be
> maintained but there are many problems . . . . In any case, I
> will be leaving the latter part of June, since the Ministry will
> appoint the new school heads.
>
> You will be surprised to know that to date our daily lives are
> deceptively ordinary. To move about the school would suggest
> nothing out of the ordinary. However, all of those things which
> people say will change are in fact being confirmed.
>
> Iran is still beautiful in the springtime, however, and Iranians
> are generally as warm and hospitable as always. Perhaps I am
> fortunate in my friends and colleagues (which is certainly true)
> but my pessimism is tempered by my daily experience of good
> sense and humanity.

There were also anguishing reports of people, of Christians,
experiencing great pain, suffering and death.[1] An educated
young wife and mother wrote to friends of the constant fear
which dominated every aspect of their life:

> . . . The middle class is the biggest loser. We are outcasts in our

own country . . . .Tell the world we are not all bad, we are not
all savages. It is so painful to suffer what we are suffering and
on top of it all to be blamed for it as well . . . .

For Jane and Gertrude, residing in a small, pleasant town,
time now seemed irrelevant. After a disciplined lifetime of daily
challenges, demands, schedules, imperatives and objectives,
spending time sitting around in a rocking chair was a bit bewil-
dering. Jane's annual report included the following observations:

> But what have I to show for the year? It has given me time to
> relax, to think, to wait upon the Lord; to rest in His promises
> and to live one day at a time. It has taught me the unimpor-
> tance of *things* and the supreme value of *friends*.

> I still receive mail from Iran and am glad to know that the clin-
> ic is still running as usual . . . . We pray that all the problems
> will indeed lead people to the Saviour Who Alone can bring se-
> curity and peace. Pray for Iran and all its disillusioned people.
> Pray for its leaders and all their problems. Pray that the Peace
> of God may enter the hearts of all men, that there be peace, un-
> derstanding and brotherhood throughout the world.

> And so—we continue to live a day at a time, not knowing how
> long we will have to remain in the United States, but constantly
> grateful for God's leading, and for the many dear friends who
> have filled the year with special blessings. God bless you all!

When Jane pondered God's leading, she remembered that:

> He that hath my commandments, and keepeth them, he it is
> that loveth me; and he that loveth me shall be loved of my Fa-
> ther, and I will love him, and will manifest myself to him (John
> 14:21).

Jane was somewhat bewildered by the present circumstances.
Time seemed to be passing her by. From her front window she
could view neighbors, often with grocery bags in their arms, on
their way to and from Main Street. The shoppers had to tred
carefully, watching for sidewalk lumps and cracks occasioned by
the forceful demands of old tree roots. Neighborhood children
scampered about, arguing over their turns on a squeaky once-red
tricycle. Others tried to play catch with an elusive yellow ball
which, their parents admonished, must be kept away from traffic
and pedestrian's feet. Sometimes a stray dog would scoot in to
chase the ball, then turn away in favor of a rollicking butterfly

race. Birds flittered past Jane's window as they lofted from the branches of the tall French lilacs to the sturdier limbs of the giant shady elms. There seemed to be plenty of action and purpose outside. But inside Jane was actively learning to "wait patiently."

On January 20, 1981, Jane and Gertrude watched in amazement and jubilation the televised celebrations featuring the return of the newly-released hostages from Iran. All Americans seemed to be united in fervent thanksgiving to God for this moment. Seated in her rocking chair, Jane thought of their much-loved home in Tehran which was less than a mile from the American Embassy. How long would it be before she and Gertrude could return to Iran?

On Inauguration Day, they watched as incoming President Ronald Reagan soberly accepted the most formidable human responsibility in the world. Jane wondered if any one human could comprehend and master the enormity of the present world needs? She shared her musings in her annual (July 1981) report to friends:

> So much to do and so little time! . . . . As an exile in the land of my birth, I find there is so much I do not know after nearly sixty years in Iran. What does one now call lump sugar, stickers, undervests (no longer existent), file folders, garment bags, etc.? Since my friend Gertrude does all the shopping, and often does not understand what I am talking about, it is important to know the present correct word! And how startling to be addressed by one's first name by everyone: casual acquaintances, the druggist, the salesmen, passersby, club women, etc., who all know us as Jane and Gertrude and probably do not know our surnames.
>
> How we miss our Tuesday afternoon callers, our car, the Iranian sunshine, to say nothing of our memorabilia, records, books, pictures, clothes and so on, still reposing in Iran and likely to remain there. Living entirely on borrowed goods makes one overly careful, but how grateful we are for the many items, large and small, which make our living comfortable, and constantly remind us of the largely unknown friends who supplied them. The thoughtfulness of friends who, among other things arrange for our transportation, is heart-warming, as well as their care and attention when both Gertrude and I were laid low by flu at Christmas time.

We are fortunate in having a fine Presbyterian Church here
which we attend regularly. Gertrude sings in the choir and I attend the adult Bible class preceding the worship service. The
very fine pastor and his wife invited us for Christmas dinner
but when circumstances prevented that, they brought us the
whole dinner . . . a real godsend since Gertrude does not cook!
For me, cooking in America has been a real problem as the
modern cookbooks give only the fancy ways to deal with food
already prepared and frozen whereas what I needed was something giving fundamental instructions. With two copies of *The
Joy of Cooking* in Iran I was finally obliged to buy a third copy
here!

Cortland is so located that friends passing by to Syracuse or
Ithaca drop in, and others have made us real visits which have
been a joy . . . . Belonging to the YWCA and the AAUW has
brought us in contact with groups of fine women whose faces
are now familiar, even if their names are not.

As requests came for me to speak about Iran to various groups,
I at first hesitated to accept, but gradually realized that many
were largely misinformed about . . . people and conditions in
Iran. Lately I have considered it a privilege to do what I could
to bring about a better understanding and appreciation between the nations . . . .

We have lived as apprentices, perhaps, preparing for the days
ahead which are all too few . . . . The clinic goes on although
now entirely under the Iranian Ministry of Health which has
moved it to a better building in the same area. They also appointed my assistant as its head, retained our entire staff, and
took over all our records and equipment.

The days rush by—so much to do—why was it not done while
we thought we had time in Iran? So little time—who knows?
Maybe the call of Islam and all its adherents now here in America is the greater challenge! Are you seeking to know them,
make friends with them, introduce them to the Living Saviour?

Gertrude, too, missed Iran every day. Iran was the country of
her birth. There was the house that Jane had built especially to
accommodate them in these years, with her own room and her
collection of Persian dolls. She yearned to see their friends, the
cool summer cottage with its luscious fruit trees, the flourishing
garden, the delicious cucumbers, the singing mountain stream,

the swift flying birds and the lively dog.

One day Jane received word that their precious little home and all its contents had been seized and locked-up by government officials! She was deeply hurt and grieved by this news. When Jane thought about it, a host of faces would stream across her memory: the poor, the needy, the sick, the house-bound, the young, the aged. And interspersed with these faces were those of the kind and caring people in America and Iran who had given of themselves and their resources for others. Slowly, steady gains had been made. But now what?

Jane comforted herself with the Iran Bethel hymn:

> I would be true for there are those who trust me;
> I would be pure for there are those who care;
> I would be strong for there is much to suffer;
> I would be brave for there is much to dare.
> I would be brave for there is much to dare.
>
> I would be friend of all the foe, the friendless;
> I would be giving and forget the gift;
> I would be humble for I know my weakness;
> I would look up, and laugh, and love and lift.
> I would look up, and laugh, and love and lift.

Resolutely, Jane and Gertrude determined to ". . . look up . . . and love and lift" in whatever work God placed before them. The geography of their lives was up to their All-wise, loving God. His commission to them was unchanged:

> What you have heard from me before many witnesses entrust to faithful men who will be able to teach others also (2 Timothy 2:2).

Every day in their exile from their beloved country, Gertrude took long walks. After a brisk walk outside, her spirits always lifted. This day, in the summer of 1981, she walked four miles to the grocery store and back. Gertrude began to sing as she placed the food on the metal table in the center of the high-ceilinged, old-fashioned spacious kitchen. Her lilting sweet soprano voice carried a melodic phrase of a hymn she'd learned long ago as a child in Tehran. Her mother had learned it when she was a young girl at Iran Bethel and she had played it often. Gertrude's father would sometimes join the musical devotion and sing out the words: "Blessed assurance, Jesus is mine . . . ."

In the living room, Jane was busy responding to questions in the letter of a seventeen year old girl who'd heard Jane speak recently: "How can a teenager be sure it's God who's calling?" the girl wanted to know. "And shouldn't you have stayed in America instead of expending yourself in a far away land where people probably didn't really care?"

Jane glanced over the lines she'd just typed in reply to the questions:

> You're young and doubtless very worldly-wise, "sophisticated" as they say. But you can think, you can see, and you can feel. (Your letter indicated all these probabilities.) So please understand—in today's society with all its pressures, tensions, noise, confusion, disappointment, defeat, it's very hard to hear the voice of God ("Be still and know that I am God . . . .") It's hard, in such a hostile environment, to even want to know God, to want to be pure, holy, honest and honorable. Who cares? Not the world—it often ridicules such qualities. But if you care (as your letter suggests), if you really want to know purpose and peace in your life, you boldly step forward to experience God! How? Believe that you are a special person (as He said), that you are loved by your Creator, God, that He has a plan for you (and all that He created). Trust in Him, commit yourself into His keeping. Pray to Him. Study His word—the Bible. Obtain a version that is helpful to you (the New International Revised is highly recommended). Get a study help (such as the Navigator's *Closer Walk*). Find other Biblical Christians in your area, express your interest and participate in a fellowship that enables you to mature in the healthful, positive way that God intends. I can assure you, your life will have more . . . .

Suddenly, the phone rang loudly. "Shall I answer the telephone?" Gertrude called to Jane.

"Yes, please," Jane answered.

As the phone continued to ring, Jane rose stiffly from her chair and walked slowly toward the kitchen.

"Gertrude! Where are you?" asked Jane in dismay. "I wonder who's so persistent?"

"Hello," said Gertrude in a breathless, cheerful voice. "Yes, this is her residence, who's calling please? . . . . Very well, she'll be here in a moment."

Gertrude laid the receiver on the small breakfast table beneath the wall phone and pulled out a chair for Jane.

"Someone from Yonkers is calling about a speaking date," she said. "I'll go get your calendar."

Jane stopped, her mind racing: "Yonkers! Around the world and right back where I started from. Our big old roomy house, my childhood home. Dad's garden . . . the sprawling pine I climbed to hide from pestering little brothers so I could read about Mary Slessor and others . . . Dad, walking the mile to church every Wednesday night for prayers regardless of the strains of the day at the office. My faithful God-honoring Dad . . . praying with me, his seventeen year old daughter, seeking God's will for my life. My loving mother, supportive, caring, selfless. O God! Thank you again for such wonderful parents, such a family and home. Am I measuring up? Have I kept the faith? Am I becoming the person You wanted me to be? Yes, Yonkers, I'll come back to share with you God's love, to tell of what He's done and is doing."

Love remembers.

Smiling, Jane seated herself carefully at the table in the kitchen. She picked up the receiver. "Hello, this is Jane Doolittle . . . "

She glanced up momentarily as Gertrude slid her calendar and pen in front of her.

"September 29?" Jane flipped the pages of her date book. "All right . . . at two o'clock? . . . You'll provide transportation and overnight lodging? . . . That'll be fine . . . . Yes, we'll bring what Persian dolls we have, though we don't have many here . . . . Yes, we'll be glad to meet you, too. We always like to tell of the people and work in Iran . . . Fine. Thank you." She hung up the phone and made a few notes for herself.

She moved back to her rocking chair and sat down. She hoped she could help this seventeen year old inquirer. Seventeen could be such a significant year. "Teenagers! How important they are. Full of energy, eagerness, willingness and enthusiasm; wanting to find the best for their lives. God help me to be a worthy guide for this young woman. Women! How tremendously significant they are to the world. What a difference it makes when women love God!"

Jane gently swayed to and fro with the rocking chair's rhythm. Forward, backward. She was caught between worlds, between

youth and age, then and now, New York and Tehran, here and
hereafter. She could feel this tug, ceaselessly. She must move on.
There was so much to do, so little time.
  "Let's not forget to take the 'chelo kebab' recipe with us when
we go this time!" Gertrude called from the kitchen. "People always want it!"
  "Yes, and they want you to bring your Persian dolls, too."
  "And our Scrabble game?" teased Gertrude. They played every night.
  Jane laughed. "Think I can't win in Yonkers?"
  "You can try!"
  The Herald Statesman of Yonkers, New York, for Tuesday, September 29, 1981, published an article about Jane Doolittle's life
and work in Iran. The article was accompanied by a candid photo taken by Staff Photographer, Robert Deutsch, during her appearance at St. Paul's Episcopal Church on Palisades Avenue,
not far from the site of Jane's family home. The photo showed a
smiling, radiant-looking white-haired lady. Was the smile on
Jane's face because perchance she was remembering when, at age
five, she'd asked her parents, "How old do I have to be before I
can pray like that?" She'd observed them in their daily 6 A.M.
devotions, kneeling beside their bed, asking for God's will and
for guidance and care of their children. Then they'd always hurried downstairs for breakfast and family devotions. Each child,
Jane remembered, had to read at least two verses of the day's
Scripture from their Bibles before Dad would rush out to catch
the commuter train to his office in New York City.
  But many long years have passed. Since then, Jane's life has
been filled with much daily praying, watching, waiting, witness-
ing, doing, accepting the hours, the news, the events as they
come. "... Thy will be done on earth as it is in Heaven ..."
Since then, illnesses and frailties have taken their toll. But the
memories are still strong.
  She thought of her home in Tehran, taken over by the Revolutionaries and emptied of all her belongings. How grateful she
was to the friends who managed to retrieve a few items precious
to Jane—her sister's paintings, her photos and her family me-
morabilia. Her dear little dog, Chippy, has been poisoned, they
said. Fortunately, Jane had given her canaries into a friend's

keeping before she left on her visit to the U.S. Her mountain cottage, they said, was robbed of all its contents. At first her friends had tried to take care of it for her, but finally it had been turned over to the church to whom Jane had previously willed it.

Ibrahim and Mahsoltan have been able to visit Jane in the U.S. and bring her news and snapshots of their family and some of her Iranian friends. Several of Jane's friends and former students have found their way to her New York residence to demonstrate again their continuing love and devotion.

Jane, at first reluctant to have her story in print, finally accepted the idea that possibly it might be a blessing to someone. Therefore, she has cooperatively assisted in this effort, as have many others who have been part of life.

If you now ask Jane to reflect upon the meaning and value of her life, or of life in general, her answers are straightforward and direct. She sits quietly in her tall-backed rocking chair. Her gaze is steady, her mind alert, her responses thoughtful.

Was it all worthwhile?

"Yes, I trust so."

Would you do it all over again?

"Yes, certainly, with fewer mistakes, I'd hope."

What do you think life is all about?

Jane leans forward in her chair. She thinks for a moment or two. "It's a person's opportunity to relate to the Creator God; to discover God's plan, to acknowledge God and to use whatever one has been given in gratitude and service to God for His love and mercies.

She settles back in her chair which sways gently forward and backward in slow movement. She continues:

"Fame and fortune are fleeting and fanciful. Our world is dying for God's love. Christians need to live out their commitment. Pretense and foolish talk are exceedingly destructive. One's words and deeds must match and show God's love—His unconditional love—for all of us, rebellious and sinful as we are. It's a big responsibility to be a Christian, to walk in the world in His name, and it's not to be taken lightly. The results of behavior that separates us from God—our sin—leads to devastation and despair. But when we repent and ask to receive God's gift, it brings joy, peace of mind, a sense of purpose and life eternal.

"Only one life to live
'Twill soon be past.
Only what's done
For Christ will last."

There's a brief pause and the rocking stops. "I wish I had done, could do, more. I still want to be counted as faithful, obedient, trusting. I have planted some seeds, but the results, whatever, are in His hand, in His time. He has provided for my needs in every situation. He sustains and comforts me as I continue to walk, albeit slowly these days, a step at a time."

She sits back in her chair and the rocking begins again. A beautiful smile illuminates her wrinkled face. With a positive lilt in her voice she states: "It's wonderful to be one of God's family, and the best is yet to come!"

From off in the distance comes Gertrude's frail, plaintive voice: "Let's go home . . . go home . . . go home . . . ."

Jane nods her head and replies softly, "Yes, I'm ready." Her chair barely moves. She looks out the big bay windows, freshly curtained by loving, caring friends. She see signs of new life, new growth, and the renewal of God's promises everywhere: the slender greening boughs, the nodding bright blossoms in Gertrude's little jewel-patch garden. "Father's garden must be beautiful, too. Each of us are seedplanters, wherever we are!"

Is love lost? Jane is at peace. To God be the Glory!

. . . My word that goes out from my mouth: It will not return to me empty, but will accomplish what I desire and achieve the purpose for which I sent it (Isaiah 55:1).

To everything there is a season, and a time to every purpose under the heavens (Ecclesiastes 3:1).

NOTES

1. See H.B. Dehqani-Tafti, *The Hard Awakening*, Seabury Press, New York, 1981. The Rt. Rev. H.B. Dehqani-Tafti, Episcopal Bishop of Iran, writes of his country's pain and of his own, including the murder of his twenty-four year old son.

Chronology:
Some Significant Events
Touching the Life
of Jane Doolittle

1897	(August 25)	Catherine Davenport Doolittle (sister) born
1899	(April 14)	Jane Elizabeth Doolittle born, Reading, PA (named for her paternal grandmother, Jane Elizabeth Sage)
		Father: Orrin Sage Doolittle (son of Edgar Jared Doolittle, Congregational Minister, Chester, CT)
		Mother: Grace Ferguson Doolittle (daughter of Nathaniel Ferguson, pig iron furnace owner, and Amanda Davenport Ferguson)
1903	(Dec. 4)	Brother, Edgar Jared Doolittle, born
1905	(July 17)	Brother, Nathaniel Ferguson Doolittle, born
		Father's business (chemical engineer with Semet Solway) moves to New York, relocates family in Yonkers, NY
1914	(June 9)	Jane is class salutatorian at Yonkers P.S.#6 (absence due to illness disqualifies her being valedictorian)
1914 - 1915		She is a five-day boarder at Bangs and Whiton in Riverdale, NY
1915 - 1917		Teenager at Capen (finishing school and preparatory for Smith College)
		At seventeen, Jane believes God is calling her to become a missionary doctor; curriculum totally changed to qualify for college entrance
1917 - 1921		Attends Wells College
	(1918)	Her friend, "the boy next door", killed in WW I
	(1919)	Attends Student Volunteer Conference, Des Moines, Iowa; signs pledge purposing to become a missionary
	(1920)	President of NY chapter of Student Volunteer Colleges Association; General Chairman, Student Volunteer Conference held at Wells College; President of YWCA; participates in hockey, science and drama clubs

1921	(Feb. 21)	In Iran, Reza Khan marches into Tehran, deposes the prime minister
	(Apr. 30)	Reza Khan becomes Minister of War and Commander in Chief of Armed Forces
	(June)	Jane is graduated from Wells College with a B.A.
	(Aug. 17)	Jane leaves for Tehran
	(Oct. 28)	Arrives at Iran Bethel ("The House of God") in Tehran (a bilingual school founded April 24, 1874 by Presbyterian Mission); Jane supported by Wells College—"Wells in Persia"—in cooperation with U.S. Presbyterian Church
1922		Organizes first girls' summer camp in Iran, twenty-six girls participate
1924	(June)	Near end of agreed-to three-year term, Jane returns home for health reasons
		First spinal fusion operation
		Studies at Columbia University and Biblical Seminary (now New York Theological Seminary)
1925	(Dec.13)	Reza Khan becomes Shah of Iran—beginning of Pahlavi Dynasty (follows Qajar Dynasty)
		Jane receives M.A. from Columbia University (in subsequent years she continues graduate work)
1926		Jane returns to Iran (in the company of Dr. and Mrs. Samuel Zwemer, great American missionary statesman whose theme was "education, not exploitation")
		Resides at Hamadan for year's language and history study
	(Nov. 10)	Brother Nat dies at Rutgers
		Father retires, continues his research, invention and gardening hobbies
1927		Jane leaves Hamadan for Tehran, becomes headmistress/principal of Iran Bethel
		Meets Gertrude Norollah at missionary conference
		Mrs. Russell Sage, of the Sage Endowment Fund, provides $200,000 to develop higher education for women in Iran
1928		The Sage College Endowment purchases property in Tehran for dormitory to house sixty girls; Persian architect works with committee from U.S. Presbyterian Board of Foreign Mission in NY
1929	(Feb.)	New building ready for occupancy
1931 - 1932		Jane in NY; has second spinal fusion operation

1932	Iranian government forces closure of all primary schools under foreign supervision
1935 (Jan. 21)	By government decree, Iran Bethel must be renamed: becomes Nurbakhsh ("Light Giving")
1936 (Jan. 7)	Abolition of the veil in Iran
	University of Tehran opens; twenty-nine women admitted in first academic year
1937 (Jan.)	Jane sent to Beirut to visit Women's Junior College; meets Winifred Shannon, Director
	Jane and Winifred snowbound while returning to Tehran
1938	Jane studies at Columbia University
1939 - 1940	Iranian government orders closure of all schools under the direction of foreign educators
	NY Presbyterian Board sends commission to Iran to cooperate in orderly transition of schools to Iranian Ministry of Education
	Jane, Gertrude and Golebehar find new residence to share
1941	Allies occupy Iran during World War II; Reza Shah forced to abdicate in favor of his son, Mohammad Reza Pahlavi
1943	Tehran Conference (Stalin, Churchill, Roosevelt)
1946	Jane returns to New York
1947	Mother stricken ill/Jane remains at home
	Bedouin shepherds find ancient manuscripts near shore of the Dead Sea ("greatest manuscript discovery in modern times")
1948	Jane returns to Tehran when her mother seems improved; her mother dies a month later
	Israel becomes a nation
	Presbyterian Board in NY allocates funds from Sage College proceeds for the Iran Bethel Project, known from 1940 as the Doolittle Project
1949	New quarters for the Doolittle Project (the need for medical assistance to women and girls had prompted Jane to open a small clinic in her own residence)
1951	Jane in NY; father becomes ill and then dies
	Family home in Yonkers is sold
1952	Jane returns to Tehran; purchases an old residence

1953		Catherine/Howard come to Iran to visit Jane
		Political power struggle in Iran
		Jane builds small summer cottage in mountains outside Tehran
1954		Cousin Amanda (Mr. and Mrs. J. Russell Craig of Philadelphia) visit Jane in Iran
1955		Golebehar dies.
		Howard dies.
1957		Catherine visits Jane for seven months and helps with art classes in the school
1958	(July)	Jane visits Catherine in NY; attends Columbia University
1959	(Dec.)	Catherine dies while Jane is with her
1960	(Jan.)	Jane returns to Tehran
1961	(Oct.)	Her brother, Jed, dies
1963		Women vote for the first time in Iran
		The "White Revolution" (no blood shed) in Iran; marriage and divorce laws modified
1964		Jane scheduled to retire; the mission board requests her to remain until a replacement is selected
		Khomeini ordered to leave Iran
1966		Jane honored at Ministry of Education party
		Jane retires from Presbyterian Mission work; Iran Bethel becomes Damavand College
		Official TV broadcasting begins in Iran
1967		Official ceremonies held for Doolittle Clinic
	(Oct. 26)	Coronation of Mohammad Reza Pahlavi as Shah and of his wife as Empress Farah
1968		Jane selected as one of ten distinguished alumnae to receive Wells College Award
		Damavand College under new administrator, Dr. Frances Gray
1971		Iran celebrates 2500th year of monarchy
1972		Jane receives citation from Ministry of Education
		Iran Bethel alumnae celebrate Jane's fifty years of service in Iran
	(June)	Jane and Gertrude move into their own small house
1975		International Decade Women of the World

1977		Islamic Revolution gains strength in Iran
	(Nov. 19)	Sadat's peace mission to Jerusalem
1979		Jane receives citation from Empress Farah
	(Jan. 17)	Shah and Empress leave Iran
	(Feb. 1)	Khomeini, leader of the Islamic Revolution, returns to Iran after fifteen-year exile
	(April 1)	Khomeini declares new Islamic Republic
	(Sept. 5)	Jane and Gertrude on scheduled visit to NY with handbags and two suitcases
	(Nov. 4)	Fifty-two Americans taken hostage in American Embassy in Tehran
1980	(Mar. 19)	In Philadelphia, Jane receives word, "Do not return to Iran"
	(June 2)	Friends of her Wells College days locate a residence for Jane and Gertrude
	(July 26)	The exiled shah dies in Egypt
1981	(Jan. 20)	American hostages released in Tehran after 444 days of captivity
	(Oct. 6)	Sadat assassinated in Egypt
1979 - 1988		Jane and Gertrude still unable to return to Iran

An Overview
of Events
in the History of Iran

Pre-History

Elamites dwell on Iranian Plateau

Pre-Islamic Period

1500 B.C.:   Medes and Persians come from Indo-Europe to settle the Iranian Plateau.

553 B.C.:   Persians of the Aechamenid Dynasty overthrow the rule of the Medes and establish the world's first great empire, stretching from the Black Sea to Central Asia and from India to Libya. For the first time, one ruler governs many different peoples. This empire was divided into provinces, each under the administration of a "satrap" (governor). Cyrus the Great, founder, practiced human rights, religious tolerance and justice. Other kings included Cyrus II; Darius, an administrative genius whose systems and procedures were adopted by later rulers of other lands; and Xerxes.

330 B.C.:   Alexander of Macedonia conquers the Persian Empire.

248 B.C.:   The nomadic Parthians, an Aryan tribe from the northeast, come into power. Their rule will last for almost five centuries.

A.D. 224:   Sassanian Dynasty—The Persian, Ardeshir (who had been the guardian of the temple of Zoroaster), establishes a period that becomes of great significance.

A.D. 642:   Arab invasions—Iran is conquered.

Islamic Period

A.D. 1005:	The Ghaznavid Dynasty (Turkish) is established.
A.D. 1058:	The Seljug Dynasty (Turkish) begins.
A.D. 1220:	The Mongols, under the leadership of Genghis Khan, crush Iran.
A.D. 1449:	The Safavid Dynasty established under Shah Ismail. The subsequent reign of Shah Abbas the Great is very significant.
A.D. 1736:	The Afshar Dynasty begins under Nader Shah.
A.D. 1779:	The Zand Dynasty established with Karim Khan.
A.D. 1787:	The Qajar Dynasty begins with Agha Mohammad Khan.
A.D. 1925:	The Pahlavi Dynasty established under Reza Shah.
A.D. 1941:	Forced to abdicate by the Allies, Reza Shah relinqishes the throne to his son, Mohammad Reza Shah Pahlavi.
January, 1979:	Mohammad Reza Shah and Empress Farah leave Iran.

Islamic Republic Period

April, 1979:	The new Islamic Republic is proclaimed by Ruhollah Khomeini, a Muslim mullah. He becomes the Ayatollah ("the sign of God").
July 20, 1980	The exiled Reza Shah dies in Egypt.

Selected Glossary
(Arabic Spelling)

ALI	A cousin of Muhammad who married the prophet's daughter, Fatima. He is highly revered by the Shi'as.
ALLAH	The Arabic name for God, chosen by Muhammad to represent the one true God.
AYATOLLAH	A sign of God.
HADITH	A collection of sayings of the prophet Muhammad.
HASAN and HUSAIN	The grandchildren of Muhammand and the sons of Ali and Fatima. Husain and his retinue were massacred at Karbala. These brothers are highly revered by Shi'as.
IMAN	A divinely appointed leader to whom Shi'as look for supernatural guidance; the leader who guides Muslims in prayers at the mosque.
ISLAM	Submission of body and soul to God.
JIHAD	A holy effort or striving for advancement of Islam and defeat of non-believers (infidels).
MUEZZIN	The man who gives call to prayer.
MUHAMMAD	Muslims believe he is the seal of the prophets through whom Allah gave His final revelation.
MUHARRAM	The name of the first month of the Muslim year. Also the name of a Shi'ite festival commemorating the martyrdom of Husain.
MULLAH	A Muslim religious teacher.
QU'RAN or QURAN	The holy book of Islam which contains the sayings of God revealed to Muhammad.
RAMADAN	The ninth month of the Muslim calendar. During Ramadan, Muslims fast from sunrise to sunset.

SHI'A or SHI'ITE   One of two main sects in Islam. The Shi'a sect believes Ali is Muhammad's designated successor and that this succession passed to twelve of his descendants through his wife, Fatima. Each of these successors is considered to be an Iman. It is believed that the twelfth Imam disappeared and remains in occultation.

SUNNI   The major sect in Islam. Sunnites accept the legitimacy of the first four khalifas. They believe the prophethood of Muhammad is final and that early systems of Muslim law are binding.

SURA   A chapter of the Quran.

Selected Bibliography

Arberry, A. J. *The Legacy of Persia*. London: Oxford University Press, 1953.

Bausani, A. *The Persians, from the Earliest Days to the Twentieth Century*. London: Elek, 1971.

The Cambridge History of Iran. Cambridge: Cambridge University Press, 1968.

Dehqani-Tafti, H. B. *The Hard Awakening*. New York: Seabury Press, 1981.

Elder, John. *The Biblical Approach to the Muslims*. Houston: Leadership Instruction and Training International, 1978.

Frye, R. N. *Persia*. London: Allen & Unwin, 1968.

The Gospel and Islam: A 1978 Compendium. Don M. McCurry, Editor. Monrovia, California: MARC, 1978.

Issari, M. A. and Paul, Doris A. *A Picture of Persia*. New York: Exposition Press, 1977.

Lewis, B. *The Middle East and the West*. London: Weidenfeld, 1964.

Livingstone, W. P. *Mary Slessor of Calabar*. New York: George H. Doran Company, Tenth Edition. (Zondervan has a recent reprint.)

Lofti, Nasser. *Iranian Christian*. Waco, Texas: Word, Inc., 1980.

Mortimer, Edward. *Faith and Power, The Politics of Islam*. New York: Random House, 1982.

Pahlavi, Ashraf. *Faces in a Mirror*. New Jersey: Prentice-Hall, Inc., 1980.

Pahlavi, M. R. *Answer to History*. New York: Stein and Day, 1980.

Pahlavi, M. R. *Mission for My Country*. London: Hutchinson & Co., 1960.

Parshall, Phil. *New Paths in Muslim Evangelism*. Grand Rapids, Michigan: Baker Book House, 1984.

Sadat, Jehan. *A Woman of Egypt*. New York: Simon and Schuster, 1987.

Saikal, Amin. *The Rise and Fall of the Shah*. Princeton: Princeton University Press, 1980.

Scott, Charles W. *Pieces of the Game*. Atlanta: Peachtree Publishers, Ltd., 1984.

Stevens, Roger. *The Land of the Great Sophy*. Great Britain: Cox & Wyman, Ltd., 1974.

Weir, Ben and Carol. *Hostage Bound, Hostage Free*. Philadelphia: Westminster Press, 1987.

Wilbur, D. N. *Contemporary Iran*. New York: Praeger, 1963.

_____ *Iran: Past and Present*, Eighth Edition. Princeton: Princeton University Press, 1976.

Williams, John Alden. *Islam*. New York: Washington Square Press, 1969.

Wysham, W. N. *A Century of Mission Work in Iran (Persia) 1834-1934*. Printed at the American Press, Beirut, Lebanon, 1936.

Young, Charlotte Elizabeth. *Memoirs and Letters of Charlotte Elizabeth Young, 1895-1982*. Private printing, 1983.

Young, Herrick B. *Strange Lands and Wonderful People*. New York: Manhattan Publishing Co., 1975.

ACKNOWLEDGMENTS

"No man is wise enough by himself"[1] and there are several people to whom I am greatly indebted for their shared talent and help:

The Issaris, Ali and Joan, their immediate and extended family, whose assistance, encouragement and hospitality have been instrumental in making this a memorable experience for me.

Jane Doolittle, and her many friends and admirers, who have graciously shared anecdotes, photos, articles, personal correspondence, time, thought and interest. I am particularly grateful to Herrick and Charlotte[2] Young, for providing material from their own private memoirs and collections; to Will[2] and Miriam[2] Wysham for many delightful conversations, useful materials and ideas; to Art and Beth Muller for their welcome suggestions and comments.

Wells College personnel who have been exceedingly helpful and cooperative, including the librarian, Marie G. Delaney, in service during my two-day campus visit, who searched and researched files and archives for material relevant to the Doolittle years.

Those who aided in manuscript preparation: Sue Palmer, who typed the first, very voluminous, outline and story; Carol Lacy, editor, who patiently and with good humor, helped me find a path through excess verbiage; Elvice McAlpine, who aided in project completion.

Joe Voorhees, my loving husband, and daughters, Sharon and Deb, who've invested hours in helping me onward and upward over mountains of books, stacks of magazines, piles of correspondence, articles and photos, and given me hope and suppo

The many others, friends of long-standing and those newly-acquired, of various faiths, races and backgrounds, who've been so cooperative and helpful (like Franck, the typewriter-photocopy proprietor, who stopped all other work to spend his whole afternoon on a rush job for me; Dick, an executive, who rescheduled his day to go hours away to shoot special photos for me; and Iraj, a student, who walked four desolate miles to make a road-emergency phone call in my behalf).

To these, and other dear pilgrims I met on this journey, my profound gratitude.

NOTES

1. Titus Maccuis Plautus (254-186 B.C.)
2. Deceased